Embodied Mastery
The Activated Activist's
Guide for Returning to Wholeness

Book One

150 Attunements and Activations

For Your Journey Towards Ascension

David Anderson Swift

Transformational Publishing ™

www.TransformationalPublishing.com

EMBODIED MASTERY
The Activated Activist's
Guide for Returning to Wholeness
Book One

Copyright © 2024

ISBN 979-8-89443-878-8

David Anderson Swift

Going Forward

You are on your journey towards Ascension. In this book, you will find Attunements and Activations designed to give you something to think about and reflect on, that will allow that journey to go more smoothly. People must realize that Ascension is a group endeavor that involves everyone living on the planet. Enlightenment is a much more personal journey of inner discovery, but Ascension is about all of us.

We either ascend together as a planet, or we don't ascend at all.

There is a Divine Plan that we all signed up for before being born, which is that someday, humanity would raise its vibrational frequency to the highest possible level and live unconditional love every day.

It means moving from our current third-density fear-based world to that of love-based fifth-density awareness, which is what each page in this book is intended to do. However, another aspect of Ascension and that of Fifth-Density Awareness is to create a whole new Earth.

Paradigms that no longer serve us are starting to fail and fall apart. Yes, it's finally happening, which means stop complaining and start the process of re-creating a whole new Earth. Humans have made a total mess of their playpen. The Bible says, in *the beginning, God created the Earth* … but God isn't going to clean it up or re-create it this time.

Re-creation is about re-creating ourselves. Everyone has undergone trauma at some point in their lives as part of their human experience, so we all become wounded sooner or later, but healing those traumas and moving beyond our emotional issues is also the human experience.

Most of the people in power are still wounded so they must feed off the energy of their supporters to hide the wound, much like a vampire would do to stay alive, but because their fear and anger issues are still there, they often do things to hurt people or themselves as an unhealthy response to feeling out of balance, out of control, and unloved.

The way to heal trauma, fear, and anger is to first identify the cause, then forgive it, release it, and replace it with a new healthy love-based behavior. That's also how to deal with old paradigms that are no longer functioning. Don't just reform it, but replace it with something entirely new, which may not exist, so be willing to create.

You came here to make the world a better place. Now is the time for us to do it, so are you willing to step outside your comfort zone?

Chances are that a little discomfort might be required to actually anchor a fifth-density timeline for a new Earth to come into existence.

Many major constructs in our world are bubbling up. They're like Alka-Seltzer does in a water glass, fizzling and shooting out rockets.

It's supposed to do that, but still, you watch it.

Re-creation is taking place before your eyes every day on the news, and when it settles, we can decide if we still need this or not.

Our world is going through massive changes in numerous things, such as education, technology, science, economics, law enforcement, health care, racism, housing, and politics, just to name a few.

Governments are not the answer. They're much too slow, totally ineffective, and lack the needed money. However, there are over 2,000 billionaires and multibillion-dollar corporations in the world that have enough money, that have the manpower, and that have the technology to repair the damage, and besides, they were the cause of most of it.

Instead of being villains, corporations can now be heroes.

After all, they are made up of shareholders, who are all just people, so all we must do is change them from a low-frequency consciousness of greed to a higher-frequency consciousness of sharing with others.

We can't continue living in a world of misuse and abuse of power.

Doing so cannot survive where only love and compassion exist.

Third density is no longer functioning the way it used to because there is now a new fifth density timeline in place which is taking over.

Therefore, the old paradigms have started to crumble, so it's going to be important to know what to replace them with because a massive do-over of everything created in fear-based third density is going to be needed to create a whole new fifth-density world.

An Activated Activist acts with love, just as acting with love creates the needed Activation. Spiritually speaking, chaos is good because it's part of the creation process, but it scares the hell out of most people.

Don't let fear take control of your life or feel as though the world might come to an end. If a construct is leaving, it's because it's not needed anymore, but do not grieve its passing. Instead, be resilient and learn to evolve because if we continue to keep putting on Band-Aids, sepsis will set in. Re-creation means *to fly or die.* It's okay that the world is crumbling, it's needed for re-creation to happen.

Remember, you are the architect of the future, but as an architect, unless you create a high road for a loving world to exist, there won't be much of a world any longer. Yes, this world could come to an end.

Remember, you signed up for this, so how you value humanity has a profound effect on the future you are creating.

Do you see humanity as redeemable and worth the effort?

You are part of the human race, so how you value others tells you a lot about how you value yourself. You are always in the process of transforming, changing, reinventing, and re-creating yourself.

Don't allow yourself to ever be limited.

A doorway has been opened for you to become the new Creator.

Someday, a new Bible will say *"When humanity had to start over, those who knew they were gods stepped up to re-create the Earth."*

This is the dawn of a whole new Earth. Everything you need to build it is already within you. If you don't think you're enough to do it, it's because you're on the wrong journey. You are here to learn how to live love every day and use that wisdom to create Heaven on Earth.

You are here to create a new world based on love.

The job of an Activated Activist is to be the change.

Introduction

Creating a new Earth based on love instead of fear will require those who can function at a very high frequency, who have resolved their fear and anger issues, who have healed their worldly traumas, and who choose to bring change to this fear-based, third-density world.

In fifth density, you don't take sides. You must listen to everyone's perspective and make loving decisions for the highest good of all.

It's okay to be involved in causes or organizations that try to create change, but for anything to be considered a function of fifth density, love must be inserted into the equation. Fifth-density activism works best as a unified group intent rather than acting on it individually and becomes most powerful when a group of loving individuals all focus on the same thing. There is no more powerful way to work towards the creation of a new Earth than for a group of high-frequency beings who intend nothing but love to think of the same outcome and direct their energy towards achieving its goal. The challenge is that there are not enough people right now who are able to function in 5-D consistently.

Many can hold that awareness for a couple of minutes, but very few are consistently that high all the time. An activated group mind is much more powerful than any individual mind because one person picks up when someone else drops off. During this time the world needs unity.

Even just three people working together make a huge difference if they focus on the same thing, otherwise, all you have is just a bunch of people all thinking and sending energy about totally different things.

For example, if a group sends energy to the rainforest as a whole it can successfully produce a result, but if each individual has a different type of tree in mind the energy will break up and dissipate.

Our world is now facing numerous multidimensional problems, and since love can travel through dimensions, those answers can be found.

In 3-D, activism calls you to choose sides. Christians are called to march against abortion, while others are called to march to support a woman's right to choose, but either way, the energy will get scattered, become a 3-D ego issue, and create frustration for everyone involved.

In 5-D, activism is neutral. The group sends energy for right action, right wisdom, right use of power, and right decision-making to leaders of both groups. If possible, you would also include their names.

Neutrality destroys divisiveness, but because of love, 5-D becomes divinely neutral. The key to divine neutrality is having the necessary compassion towards yourself to admit you don't know everything.

In divine neutrality, you are awake because you trust the Universe, but to be activated in 5-D means you have gotten off the couch and are now asking others to trust the Universe as well. If enough people on the planet choose love over fear, it will open a portal for multidimensional answers to be found, and then a new Earth can be created.

The majority of mass consciousness creates the consensus reality, but you only need 25% to change the minds of the majority.

Fifth-density activism puts it out to the Universe for those in power to make right choices for the highest good of all, without taking sides, and educating others to trust that the Universe is smarter than they are, which will open doors for what best serves you, humanity, and Earth.

Our world is in the middle of a revolution, but we don't want it to get violent. Instead, we want to create a consciousness revolution.

Courage without a sword is the ultimate goal of a spiritual warrior.

Chaos and crises are happening more frequently for a good reason.

It's not a sign of any failure on your part, nor the fault of humanity.

You see more turmoil and disasters because you're succeeding at doing the work, and growing, which is causing everything to change.

So stop taking sides, work in unity with focused intent, always try to adopt an attitude of divine neutrality, and live love every day.

1

As a human, you live in a third-density world, so you *'fall in love,'* which is why so many relationships fail, but once you make the shift out of 3-D and into 4-D, you become a divine human and *'fly in love.'*

When you cross the bridges of belief and can release your past, then everything about you and your world will begin to change. Remember, once you become a butterfly, you never go back to being a caterpillar.

2

It's time for the human race to quit running around in circles going nowhere. Get yourself off the hamster wheel of the rat race. Transform, stand up, and learn to say "No" to those who feed you their crumbs. Become what reflects your true nature. It's time to focus on creating a whole new world. Join the Light race, for together we can be greater, together we can be stronger, and we can experience love together.

3

Something profound is beginning to take place all across the planet. Listen carefully, close your eyes, and focus your attention so that you can hear the sound of a different drum beating in the wind, then follow it and see where it leads you. Doing so could be the most important decision you've ever made, in this or any other lifetime.

4

Do not be fooled, you are all warriors, and you know it. You are warriors of old who have returned at this time of great change to help stabilize all the new energies that are coming in, to hold the doors open, to act as an anchor for those desiring to leave third density, and to assist their weary souls through. It's what you've always done. So learn to channel your inner Divine Warrior Goddess, set your vision with love, create your goals, lead the way, and start working towards and teaching others to create a whole New World. Let nothing stand in your way.

5

With every situation in life, we're faced with making right choices. We must choose right action, right wisdom, and right decision making, to react with fear or to respond with love. It is a Third Ray function of Source involving intelligent activity and active intelligence. Each day, send your loving energy to the leaders of our world so that they can make use of this Third Ray. The survival of this world depends on it.

6

When faced with a triggering situation, it's better to respond rather than react. With a reaction, we are usually in survival mode (our ego) and our mind is on autopilot. It's because our mind becomes focused on fear, causing us to fight, flee, or freeze. A loving response can occur if we have taken the time to think about it intelligently. Whenever you feel yourself being triggered, first just try to be still and take a good deep breath. Then consider the situation thoroughly before speaking or moving forward. Always try to do the best you can with what you have available to you at any given moment. Meditation practice can help you learn not to react to situations immediately. When you add love to your responses, unfathomable doorways will always open.

7

Crop circles are not created by aliens. Earth itself is communicating with us in the language of sacred geometry, just as she does in nature. The messages are here to remind us that Earth is a living, sensual being. The circles are telling us to slow down and take time to admire the beauty this planet has to offer. If this is to be your last lifetime on Earth, you should want to experience every bit of her splendor. As it is said, "you may never walk this way again" … so don't miss this opportunity.

8

Life is only as crazy and scary as you allow the illusion to be, and the biggest mistake anyone can make is to believe the illusion they live in is real. Instead, learn to practice having non-judgment, detachment, and Divine Neutrality in everything you do. Divine Neutrality means you're not allowing yourself to get triggered by the illusion. It doesn't mean you're just floating haphazardly like a school of jellyfish. Instead, you are out in the world trying to make it better by acknowledging that each of us has our own imperfections, which is truly quite beautiful.

9

Two major paradigms must be changed before a New World can be created; to heal our wounded selves and to bring a final end to racism. Even those who thought they'd healed their wounds many years ago didn't do enough. The wounded masculine is destroying both humanity and this planet and the wounded feminine is lacking in love. Racism has its tentacles deeply embedded in all of the other paradigms and is born from the wounded feminine. It arises because you think you're not perfect and don't love yourself enough, but everyone who lives in 3-D feels imperfect, so learn to be okay with that. The Divine Masculine puts wings on love and learns to fly. The Divine Feminine knows that everyone is worthy of love and puts that wisdom into the mind of mass consciousness. When both our inner and outer expressions of love are functioning properly, racism will no longer exist. When you are finally able to say, "I don't know you, but I'm here for you, and I love you," it will literally change everything about this world.

10

Three out of five major religions created a god that sits on a throne at the top of a pyramid scheme without a female counterpart sitting by his side … those being Christianity, Judaism, and Islam. Goddess was betrayed, imprisoned, and hidden by god-fearing masculine energy but her loving shadow remained within their religious legends. This is why we say that the energy of Goddess is coming back, although she never actually left. She's always been there, but this time she will be different. Goddess was never meant to be a doormat. Love is not something you can just turn on and turn off like a faucet of angry tears, true love always loves, even when Goddess must put on her warrior's face.

11

The spiritual evolution of humanity should be at the forefront of what we all strive for in life, however, our awakening to enlightenment is being challenged by the potential trappings of the new technology which wants to replace human consciousness with computer-generated consciousness that would not only speed up learning but could even think and solve puzzles, like an artificial brain. But that is just a scam. Its real objective is to create a cloud of artificial realities designed to manipulate your beliefs and take your money. If humanity isn't careful, the new technology will become like a new god and rob you blind.

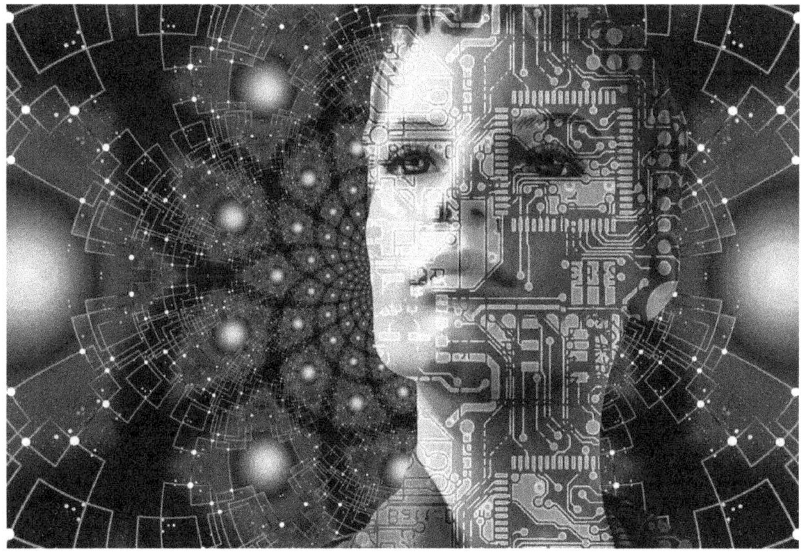

12

If your goal is to create a conscious awareness of your 'I Am Self' (your own god within) then that's where your primary focus should be, but to become a Divine Human, one must first heal their wounded self, both their masculine and feminine aspects. Once the majority of the people on the planet, i.e., *mass consciousness*, have done that as well, our awareness of consciousness will be like a whole new intelligence that we can call, N.I., by intuitively connecting into the cloud of the collective mind so that humanity can function together as one heart, one mind, and one body. Otherwise, with A.I. we become like a hive. Everyone must realize that N.I. can be achieved without A.I. and that a whole New World based on love and compassion can then be created.

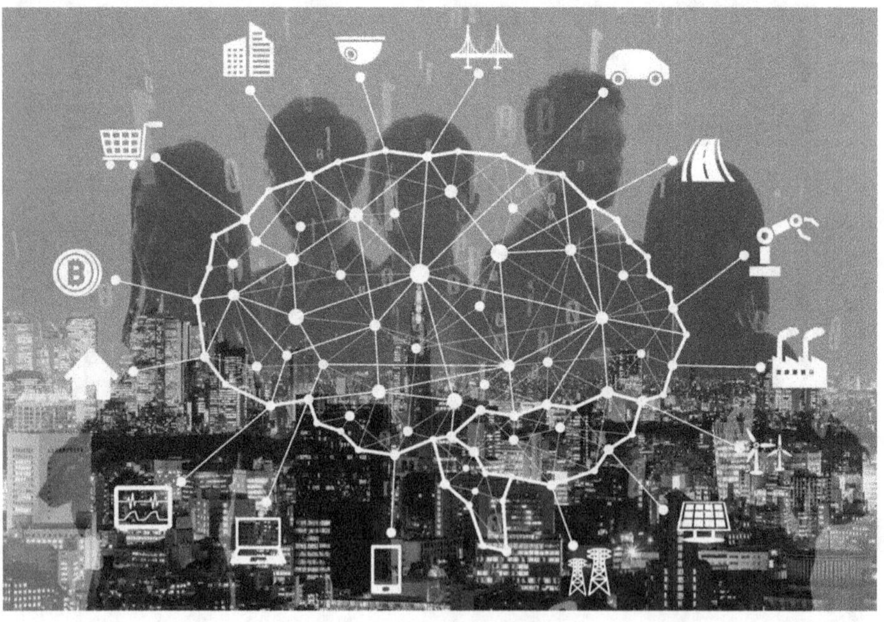

13

Your ego-personality represents 'who you are' with a human mind, which you present to the world, and is expressed as your connection to mass consciousness, but your true nature is 'what you are' as a Spirit, which you present to the world, and is expressed as your connection to All That Is. You want to be in constant awareness of both *who you are* and *what you are.* You want to bring an end to any sense of separation by bridging the gap between Heaven and Earth, or Human and Spirit.

14

The energies of this third-dimensional reality are reflective, which means everything you experience is a mirror of something going on within yourself because you try to understand energy based upon what you already know, but the reflection brings up feelings of separation, so fear is created ... therefore, most of us function in life being in either fight, flight, or freeze mode, which has to do with survival of the ego. The problem is, that the ego is a self-created illusion, so there is nothing to protect. Think of it this way; the first time you walk in outer space you feel scared because you're floating in the air with no place to put your feet, but after a while, you realize … you don't need the ground to stand on. That's the nature of the ego and your relationship to fear. That's also the attitude we must adopt to shift out of 3-D and into 4-D.

15

To say "I'm only human" is no longer a valid excuse for not being able to control your emotions … feeling angry, losing your temper and being hateful, or doing harm to others. It's time to get yourself together and begin acting like a Divine Human in this world. It's not that hard. Practice doing it like you would an orgasm … fake it until you make it.

16

What humans fear most is *the lake of the unknown,* which is change, but change is the only thing you can depend on. In Buddhism it is said, *the only thing that is real is change*, and it's happening all of the time, but you should welcome change into your life because it creates chaos, and it's within the energy of chaos that the magic of transformation and growth works best. Any hope for creating a positive future is going to require massive change because first, we must remove old paradigms. Remember, out of chaos comes an opportunity for unlimited potential.

17

If you're going to be a pathfinder, a way-shower, and a lighthouse for others to find their way in the darkness, be prepared for obstacles and even stumble over them at times. On the road to moving humanity from 3-D to 4-D, there will be many problems to overcome, but even in 4-D, there will still be boulders along the way. Our job is to learn to overcome whatever obstacles that might show up in our quest to create a whole New World. But remember, everything you experience is an aspect of you, so as you allow yourself to heal, you also heal the world.

18

In 1966, Dr. Karl Menninger wrote, *The Crime of Punishment* to show the world that incarceration was ineffective in reducing crime. Since then, The Pugh Institute for Justice has proven this to be true in numerous studies. In 1862, Victor Hugo wrote *Les Misérables* to show that an ex-convict could forever be changed by showing compassion. In 1886, Leo Tolstoy wrote, *The Death of Ivan Ilyich* to show that we must question everything we now believe to be true about our criminal justice system. The energy of change is here, so it's time to reconsider how we view offenders. Instead of demanding some sort of payback, retribution, and punishment, we need to show love, compassion, and kindness. For most of them, we should always seek an alternative to incarceration. Old paradigms must shift, to create a whole New World.

19

We think we live in a broken world because of the reflective nature of third density, so everything seems to be backward, like in the story, *Alice in Wonderland*. As soon as she went through the mirror, her world became topsy-turvy. When the Spirit that you are came into your body, what you saw was a mirror image of your true self. Because of that, what you believed to be true was often the reverse of what it should be, fear instead of love, anger instead of joy, darkness rather than Light, hatred instead of compassion, an ego instead of non-ego, fragmentation instead of wholeness, and you felt bound to time instead of no time, but the world is only as broken as you are, and will continue so long as you allow it to be. We must learn to heal both our wounded masculine and wounded feminine selves, which can be done by living love every day. Remember that to ascend, you can't take your old 3-D self with you.

20

Everyone would like to think they are already living in 4-D or 5-D, but how do you know? The test is not about how good you are or what nice things you've done. The true test is about how angry you still get, how fearful you are of the world, how frustrated you are with life, and how upset you still become when something goes wrong. Look closely at how you react to the illusion. If you're still stuck in the swamp of your ego, then you're still in 3-D. How do you get out of quicksand? You take a deep breath, lay back, release your panic, and your fear of dying … then allow yourself to float to the top gently and slowly.

21

We are in a time of major transition, moving from 3-D to 4-D, and will eventually enter 5-D. The caterpillar is like a slug that is in 3-D. The chrysalis is like being in 4-D, the time of transformation, and the butterfly is like being in 5-D, which is about freedom consciousness. The chrysalis represents the transition when one is no longer an actual caterpillar or a fully formed butterfly. It's no longer on the ground and not yet safely able to fly … but do not be in fear this time of transition. Don't ever fear anything the Universe offers you. It's all your energy, it's all for you and all about you, and surely…you don't fear yourself.

22

The tribes are being called to come together and to take the high road, to leave the past behind, and to live love every day in peace … so find your clan, the one that best fits your frequency, and build communities for a whole New World. The key to creating a successful future is for us to work in unity, the many functioning as one. That requires letting go of your ego, your anger, your trust issues, and your fears. Like it was said in the Sixties ... you're either on the bus, or you're off the bus. When the alarm clock goes off to wake you up, don't hit the snooze bar.

23

There was once a man facing a firing squad who didn't seem to care. An officer of the regiment asked, "Why is it that you do not fear death?" The prisoner just smiled and said, "Because, I'm not attached to life."

24

In the last few years, we've certainly seen a lot of death, and we are all grieving in one way or another. Life is indeed very precious so each of us should appreciate every minute we are here. Anyone who is afraid of dying is too attached to their ego and takes death much too seriously. Death should not be feared, it's organic and natural, something you've all experienced thousands of times before. You cannot leave this Earth until your Soul chooses to open that window. It's an inner choice that you can feel, so when it opens, welcome it, but as long as that window remains closed, there's no way in hell you're going to fall out of it, however, make sure it's a portal, otherwise you won't be able to leave. Just saying, *I'm tired of this and don't want to be a part of it anymore,* won't be enough, but if there is a point where your work is over you will be able to go. Dying isn't hard. Living is the challenge. When it's your time, tell your body what's happening, like you're talking to your beloved dog, *here's what's coming up, I need to do this, and here's why.* Talk to your spirit self. When you have a portal, it's simple. When you don't have a portal, it can be pretty messy. So know before you go.

25

The physics of 3-D involves reflective energy that creates a feeling of separation from Source that causes insecurity and fear for your ego. The physics of 4-D is a much more expansive energy, so the feeling of separation decreases. For example, your concept of time changes as the past, present, and future seem to come together. In 5-D, which is what all of us should be moving towards, there is no separation whatsoever, only wholeness…but the journey into 4-D and then into 5-D just can't happen if you're still attached to your ego, still caught up in your fears, still getting angry at yourself and others, still not loving yourself, and still worried about dying. Trust the Universe and learn to let go of this old fear-based paradigm, take a big step forward…and just walk on.

26

Most of our current institutions are fear-based constructs created for the survival of the ego, but as we begin to realize our Oneness and our interconnectedness with the rest of the life-force energy on the planet, we feel inclined to create new paradigms that are better suited for our new awareness and more expansive, by having their foundations firmly grounded in love and compassion. It's important to remember that it's not about reforming the old, it's about creating something entirely new. Be like the mythical Phoenix, die to the old, so the new can rise again.

27

The Avataric message we were given for 3-D nearly 2,000 years ago was to *love your neighbor as yourself*. The new message for 4-D is to *live love every day*. The message for 5-D will be *to love all, always*. The difference between 4-D and 5-D is that to *live love every day* is something you do, but to *love all always* is more like a state of being. That's the ultimate lesson … learning to 'just be' what you already are.

28

I wrote a novel about my life growing up in the turbulent Sixties when the United States was having a true consciousness revolution, and because history repeats itself, it's a book that sheds light on what the youth of today are facing. One reason the 'peace & love movement' didn't succeed was that many of them resorted to violence. They were against the war, the military draft, and the government. For peace and love to prosper, one must never be against anything, instead, to be for everything. In other words, don't be against war, just be for peace. Don't be against hate, just be for love. Don't be against the government, just be for good government. That's how a New World will be created.

29

If you fear death and loss, you'll also fear losing your wounded self, but remember, your wounds are the world's wounds, and your healing is needed to pave the way for the world's healing. It's easy to believe that *bad shit happens every day*, but you must keep moving forward. Breathe deeply as often as you can, don't get caught up in the illusion of fear and frustration, and just ride the river to see where it takes you. That so-called *bad shit* could be the door to a wonderful new beginning.

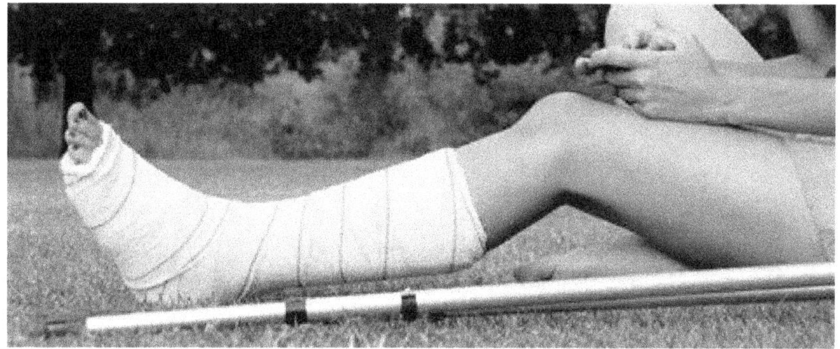

30

Our 3-D experience has been a fear-based reality for the last 12,000 years, since the days of Atlantis, but the timeline for 4-D will be much shorter because it's sort like a loading platform of a train station where we make the switch from 3-D into 5-D … it's the chrysalis that allows the caterpillar to become a butterfly. But to get there, we must heal our wounds, release our attachments to the past, forgive, trust the Universe, have hope for humanity, and have faith in ourselves. Living love every day in 4-D and doing the best we can with what we have available, prepares us to successfully function in 5-D … and 'love all, always.'

31

These days, a lot of people still believe that we are on the verge of a 'great war' between the light and the dark, good against evil. I would say it this way … the only war that exists, or ever will be, is the war going on within yourself, between your own light and dark, and your interpretation of good and evil. In the big picture, there is no sin or evil. The whole concept of sin arose because of the reflective nature of 3-D, which creates a feeling of separation from Source. The more separate from God we feel, the more we believe in things like darkness and evil. Remember, light and dark both come from the same original source and are just perspectives. The only war that is happening is the one taking place inside of you, and to win that one ... would certainly be great.

32

Many people believe that God made them unique and have trouble understanding how past lives can fit into that. It doesn't matter if you believe in reincarnation, what does matter is knowing 'who and what' you are in this lifetime. Our sense of uniqueness comes from the feeling of separation we have in 3-D. Because the energy is reflective, we feel fragmented, limited, and not enough, but our human self is just a small piece of our bigger picture. Think of past lives as aspects of you that function to create balance and wholeness, which together work to patch up the holes in this lifetime. There's also your Higher Self, Future Self, Soul, and Entity Self. A big galactic party is happening all around you, which is being held by you, one that celebrates you 'waking up' in this lifetime and becoming whole. *Everything happening is all about you.*

33

Today I was in the ocean floating on my back staring at an open sky, which reminded me of enlightenment because it has that same quality. It's a word that's hard to discuss or even define because it has no walls, boundaries, borders, or barriers. The moment you try to describe it, you're putting it into a box that can't hold it. Therefore, one can only say what enlightenment is not or what it's similar to. The word itself originated 2,800 years ago after Buddha sat under a tree for 7-weeks, then had a miraculous realization. The only role model we have in our culture like that is Jesus, and since meditating for months or being hung on a cross to die isn't what most of us aspire to, many people are not sure what to do. But thousands of years have passed, and by now our understanding of consciousness has changed so you must let go of those outdated stereotypes. Just know that when you do attain enlightenment, it won't be anything at all like you thought it was going to be.

34

By understanding the reflective nature of 3-D you can learn what is meant by bringing an end to duality. It's about releasing the feeling of separation to experience *the many*, which is your multidimensional self. You become more in touch with your creativity and can feel sensuality like never before. Facing *the many* is like gazing into a crystal ball that provides you with a pure reflection of what you are. The realization of enlightenment is that you are so much more than just a physical body with a personality ego, so much more than anyone could ever imagine. The release of duality begins to happen as we move into 4-D awareness. The reflective nature of 3-D acts like boxes, borders, boundaries, and barriers that create the illusion of separation, but they begin to fade as you enter 4-D because your concept of time changes. As the veil of the illusion begins to lift … past, present, and future start to come together.

35

Realms, planes, and dimensions are density shifts of energy that are intertwined and overlap each other. First density is basic life awareness (minerals & plants). Second density creates personal identity awareness (animals). Third density is security-oriented, fear-based ego awareness (humans). Fourth density is like a runway that's needed before we take off and begin to fly. It's also where the roots of love begin to take hold. Fifth density is the mastery of the Light Body and the discovery of your multidimensional self. It's also about being of service to those who are coming into fourth. Sixth density is the last expression of ego from your most recent lifetime. It happens in the realm of death before your next incarnation. You are always in the process of ascending, but conscious ascension means you're actively working to make this your last lifetime on Earth. If you're successful, the cycle is broken so that incarnations on Earth come to an end ... however, Embodied Ascension before death is now becoming possible. Seventh density is where all of your former aspects come together in wholeness. Densities eight, nine, ten, eleven, and twelve are not about you, but the planets, stars, and galaxies.

36

Fourth density has two parts, lower and upper. 'Waking up' occurs in lower fourth but traces of fear-based ego still exist. If you realize your core issues, seek truth, live in harmony, and trust the Universe, you'll manifest what's needed to overcome this by stabilizing your thoughts and feelings, which shifts you into upper fourth and activates you into service for others. In lower fourth, third density experiences begin to transform into wisdom and loving-kindness, so just as water is soaked up like a sponge, upper fourth absorbs and expands itself like that until you are 'living love' every day and eventually make the shift into fifth density. There are very few in mainstream consciousness who have reached upper-fourth density awareness but that will soon change. For now, billions of people are stuck, temporarily experiencing the love of lower fourth, then slipping back into their old fear-based patterns. What's needed is to have more in fifth density to act as anchors and to hold them steady, so they don't keep slipping back into third density.

37

It seems at times that everyone in the world is suffering from PTSD, running as fast as they can in fear, not knowing what they're afraid of. They keep stuffing their little cheeks just in case there's a bad winter, but there's no need to do that, and you certainly don't want that sort of thing happening in your New World. The human rat race normalizes behaviors and beliefs that cannot continue any further, like depression, desperation, loneliness, separation, hoarding, insecurities, and a sense of inferiority, always wanting more in ways that show up as a lack of sensitivity, passion, and compassion. The hamster wheel of life creates deep-seated anger and anxiety that show up on the surface as abuse, addiction, judgment, fear of being judged, and an unwillingness to try something new, which is not the timeline you want to be on. Depression is not the natural way for you to function. Your natural self is Divine and always functions best with love, compassion, and non-judgment.

38

Like many religions, sometimes those who believe themselves to be 'woke' develop a snobbish sense of elitism and entitlement, claiming they just can't be in another person's low vibrational energy. It's one thing to set boundaries to protect yourself from abuse, but it's totally different to think you're better than others by perpetuating the problem of separation. In Buddhism, initiates take a vow to be the last person on Earth to attain enlightenment, which means to release the trappings of the ego and to realize we are here to help others attain enlightenment. Developing an attitude of self-empowerment and sovereignty doesn't mean dumping your family and friends or hide from the world. In fact, it's the opposite, because in third density the ego is all about 'me' but in fourth density, you begin to shed the ego, so instead it becomes all about 'we.' Remember the song, Hey Jude, by the Beatles. *"You know that it's a fool who plays it cool by making his world a little colder."*

39

Humans tend to be overly materialistic, constantly seeking rewards, which creates beliefs about the afterlife. Religion teaches that if we are good humans we will be rewarded by God and go to heaven but even the non-religious who claim to be down-to-earth spiritual people also tend to believe there's some kind of bonus waiting for them after death. In the afterlife, you don't go home and get handed a chocolate cookie. You're already home right now and you have the cookie in your hand. You have the gift of life, which allows you to experience the sensuality of the Earth realm. Souls are standing in line waiting to come to Earth, so isn't just being here a reward enough? Don't let spiritual materialism keep you from being happy and joyful. Being depressed, stressed out, or worrying about what might happen is such a waste of the short time you have here on Earth. You are the Universe, which allows you to be the creator of your reality. Everything you experience is all about you.

40

Every human has something to offer the world that no one else can because each of us has a unique gift. To create new paradigms and have a New World, we must use the gifts we have and play whatever roles are required. The planet only has about thirty years left to get back into proper alignment before it becomes unsustainable, which is different than climate change. It simply means that humanity has been acting like a bunch of children for a very long time and has made a huge mess inside their playpen, which must be cleaned up to manage the world's population. Those who are awake must get off their couches and begin creating massive change. We have the capability, and the work force, and the money, and the technology, but old paradigms must be wiped completely clean for a true reality shift to happen. A whole New World will require the love of Divine Feminine energy for creative inspiration, and the wings of Divine Masculine energy to give it flight. Become so inspired that you're willing to fly and help clean up the world's mess.

41

The decade we've just begun is crucial for both humanity and Earth, so don't waste your time dealing with a lot of your old karmic issues, let go of them now. When a gardener's plants come up there are often weeds and grass taking up space so they must be removed to make e room for the more important plants to grow. Let go of all of your crap, because you won't be able to take it with you into a whole New World, so get down to the business at hand, to bring Earth back into balance so that humanity can fulfill the Plan for Ascension, which is to 'live love' at the highest possible vibration. However, Ascension is not just for humanity alone, but for the Earth and all life force upon it. We are all a part of the same experiment, and it will take all of us to make it work.

42

Ascension is like a series of doorways where you go from smaller rooms into larger rooms. Fifth density is a vast room which is a function of one's spiritual energy because it's grounded with the energy of love rather than fear. Even in lower fourth density, there is still some fear but that leaves as you move into upper-fourth, so fourth acts more like a bridge, a transition that provides you with the practice of 'living love' before actually reaching fifth. At the moment, there are very few people on the planet consciously functioning in fifth density awareness but that is quickly shifting. When there are enough, massive change will begin to happen that some will say are 'the fulfillment of ancient prophecies.' Divine Neutrality and unconditional love are what's needed by those in fifth to anchor the ones coming into fourth from slipping back into the old fear-based energies, otherwise, these so-called 'prophecies' could become negative instead of positive. After all, the word 'apocalypse' means, *lifting the veil*, and what's being lifted is the veil of separation, but to people who are still in fear, such an event would be frightening.

43

If the word 'brain' means something that causes us to react, feel, think, or express an emotion, then we have three brains … in our head, gut, and heart. There are more neurotransmitters in our gut and heart than in our head, and more serotonin and dopamine. That's why eating makes us feel better when we're stressed, or just receiving a hug will help to relieve depression. The head brain catalogs our experiences then analyzes them, then applies logic to mental functions going on in our present moment. It also controls certain body functions. The gut brain is about survival, understanding our identity, and our role in the world. It includes the microbiome found all over the body and influences our behavior and intellectual functions, and controls bodily functions based upon past experiences. The heart brain senses energy and maintains our emotional function based upon our future hopes, trust, faith, and love. Spirituality and intuition are associated with the pineal gland, which is not a brain but is more like a window that regulates the amount of light coming into our body, much like a third eye for all three brains to use, so the pineal must be clear, not just for health, but to keep our psychic connections functioning properly. For example, putting fluoride in our drinking water is thought to be harmful to the pineal gland, which could explain why so many people are having trouble meditating these days.

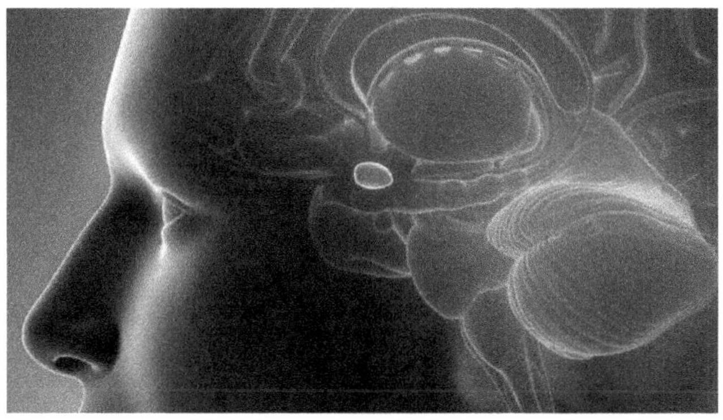

44

The energy of love creates a portal that transcends all dimensions. You're here to change the world but you can't always control what you experience, only how you experience it. Changing how you perceive the world requires healing your wounded self by dealing with all your old traumas, shame, anger, and fear. Doing so allows you to perceive yourself through the eyes of love, but until you fully love yourself you don't have the love that's needed to change the world. When you fully love yourself you're functioning in fifth density. The love you put out to the world acts as an anchor for those still in the fear-based energy to pull themselves up into fourth density and eventually into fifth density. Self-love involves the use us all three brains, the head, heart, and gut, so be aware of these as you go through your day. When you feel bad or sad ask yourself … *where am I hurting, why am I hurting, and how do I deal with my hurt?* You can't get rid of anything until you replace it with something else, so try to find ways to replace your hurt with love.

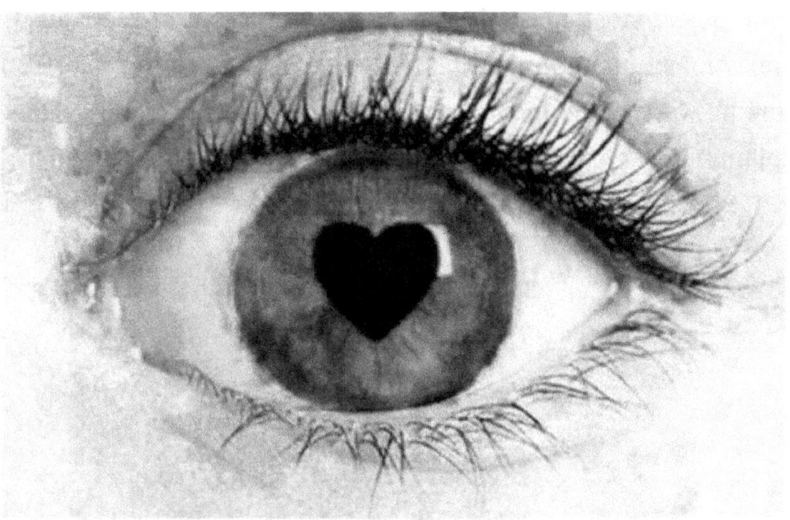

45

Waking up is Divine Feminine energy associated with *Activation*, which is Divine Masculine energy, and both are needed. Many spiritual teachers will tell you that for Ascension, all you must do is sit on your couch and listen to them talk, which often requires paying them lots of money, but I say otherwise. To sit on your lotus blossom trying to attain enlightenment is old energy. You are here at this time in history when massive change is needed to create a whole New World … one which includes almost all paradigms. To that will require Divine Humans who are Awake and Activated, wanting to get out of bed every day as though they have love with wings and the motivation needed to take it into the streets … but Activated Activists shouldn't get themselves stressed out, carry a cross, or a gun, or fight for a one-sided political cause. Rather, they must always maintain divine neutrality and be consciously aware that literally, everything they do affects everyone else.

46

Everything you do is either an act of love or fear, and the difference can be subtle, like a wolf in sheep's clothing. Even when you drink a cup of coffee, is it an act of love because it's healthy, or the fear you'll get tired? Are you in a relationship because of love, or is it convenient? The worst thing any human can do is to become occupied and satisfied, to become complacent and content, to stop moving forward out of the fear you might lose some comfort. Always try to remain at least a few steps outside your comfort zone and be willing to feel uncomfortable. For real change to happen this might be needed. New paradigms are coming, but as the old ways start to crumble, things could be unpleasant for a while. Remember Frodo, from Lord of the Rings, who was scared to leave the Shire until he found the courage to step beyond it and began his journey to release the Ring of Power (the ego). It felt scary at times, but a whole New World opened up and changed his life. The Universe is in a state of constant expansion. You are that Universe, which is what Ascension is about, your willingness to courageously expand into love no matter what difficulties or obstacles are in the way. Be like Frodo.

47

The most courageous people are those willing to look in the mirror and see the truth about themselves, to face their darkness, their traumas, their prejudices, and where they are stuck. Everything on the planet is changing faster than ever before and will continue to do so throughout this decade, but because the veil of separation is being lifted, you can influence that change. All energy is neutral, but we put labels on energy based on our experiences, mostly painful, fear-based ones. However, in fourth density, we'll insert love into that equation. This is why you are here, why you were born during this time of great shift, which is to become a Divine Human and create a whole New World. The time to act is now, which is the only time there is. The energies coming in are so powerful that our DNA is altering, death isn't what it used to be, and even Ascension is changing, but for us to experience these kinds of new paradigms requires transformation and conscious awareness of how we feel on the inside and the outside. Our wounded feminine must become Divine Feminine. Wounded masculine must become Divine Masculine. A Divine Human loves themself completely, always strives to do the best they can with what they have available at the moment and makes it their focus to shine their light and consciously live love every day.

48

The manifestation process for humans uses four steps, in this order, Intent, Thought, Word, and Deed. Colombus Day is when the deeds of a famous explorer are celebrated, but that event is being challenged and slowly becoming *Indigenous Peoples Day.* Old paradigms like this are crumbling because the original intent wasn't based on love but was about conquering new lands and those living there. Colombus was very brave and faced many hardships to get where he was going and when he got there he was met by friendly, trusting people. Had his intent been to learn from them, to touch in with curiosity to see who they were, and to leave the power with those who were already there, history would be a lot different. If the intention of his voyage had been a function of love and unity, rather than ego, our world would not be the same as it is now. Let this be a lesson as we go forward and create our own New World. Remember to set your intentions to that of love, compassion, and unity. Doing so will create a solid base that will last for thousands of years.

49

A whole New World must be new, including how you relate to it. Don't assume you'll receive the same amount of love you're giving to others because most people aren't capable of returning love in that way. Be careful thinking that you deserve a reward, or that you're entitled to go to Heaven, it's just your ego all caught up in spiritual materialism. Avoid expectations that might not be based on what's really going on. Despite the limitations of deserving, expecting, and receiving, our task is to create new paradigms by living love every day. As you seek new and creative ways to bring a whole New World into existence, try to remember that most people want to keep the wisdom of the old without the pain that came with it, so they just reform instead of creating new, but they'll accept new ways of doing things and adapt much quicker so long as it's realistic enough that their minds can actually imagine it.

50

The year 2021 was a time of incubation, and 2022 was the beginning of a coming-out party that should last for at least ten more years and will be a time for those who are Awake and Activated to come together in unity, to put aside their differences, and merge their energies in order to repair the damage that's been done to the Earth by new technologies. The goal is to build new sustainable communities based on love, but it requires a motivation stronger than a lion's roar, a giant tidal wave to create a tsunami of chaos that can wash away the old so new seeds can be planted, allowing the transformation needed for a whole New World to begin, so make yourself ready now and be prepared to ride that wave.

51

There's a difference between being unique and exceptional because we are all unique, just like everyone else, but to believe you are unique creates a feeling of separation. In the bigger picture, we are not separate from Source or each other, but each of us is exceptional because there's something you can do better. Some sing better than others, swim better, fly better, dance better, or tie their shoes better. Have you discovered your exceptional gift? If not, find it, you could have more than one. These are the gifts you were born with to help others on this planet and are the same gifts that will be needed to create a whole New World.

52

The foundation for 3-D is fear-based and is always in survival mode creating the perception that your ego is something real. Not only does it make you feel separate from others, but you always ask the question, *am I enough, do I have enough, can I do this?* You created your ego between the ages of 1 to 7 to survive. As you move into higher densities the ego begins to dissolve because it was never real, to begin with, but the love you are doesn't dissipate because it transcends dimensions, and the higher you go on the spiritual ladder the stronger your love will get. In the Age of Pisces, it could take an entire lifetime to release your ego, but in this New Age, and with the new energies that are here, you can release your ego much more quickly. That's what it means to begin making yourself ready for the future. It's not about stockpiling food, supplies, and weapons out of fear. It's about letting go of those fears, feeling safe, expressing compassion, and being consciously aware if you are reacting to the illusion we call life … or responding with love.

53

When predicting human behavior, psychologists fail to consider the stupidity factor. It may not be a good choice of words but just admit it, humans are stupid, look at the news. Some say the reason humans exist at all is that God became disappointed with the monkeys. Now, God is disappointed with humans. Most of us still carry the Neanderthal gene, and some have up to 20%, but natural changes are taking place in our DNA that involve activating previously unused genetic codes to replace the old stone age genes to be more crystalline-like. As we gently move from a carbon-based body into a silica-based body, and as these new DNA codes start to light up, we'll be able to experience our Light Body. The potential for experiencing such a body has always existed, but as we get closer to fifth-density awareness, the more it becomes a reality. When the majority of humans on Earth are consciously 'living love' every day, instead of remaining Homo-sapiens, a whole new species of Light-sapiens will emerge as the wisdom bearers for the future.

54

Working in unity brings change easier and faster because it amplifies your connection to the Source Field. With any group you are part of, all that's needed is just a small percentage of the collective to send out massive energy for change. As long as love is the foundation, putting your focus together with others of similar spiritual intent, means there's no limit to what you can create or how many you can reach because the energy of love transcends dimensions and attracts other beings who are not in form. With personal intent, group intent, and intent of the unseen, these higher frequencies working in unity create a quantum vibration of love throughout the Universe generating enormous waves of energy composed of positive particles that knock down the walls of fear-based paradigms that have existed for thousands of years. Just as the Israelites knocked down the walls of Jerico with blasts of their trumpets, we are here to do the same thing on a much larger scale, but without violence. In the Age of Pisces, changes took place one by one. For this New Age, to create a whole New World requires unity, the many with the many.

55

Humans are creator beings. When you see things in your experience that seem to be broken, divisive politics, threats of war, or any fear of future disasters, realize … this is not where you want your focus to be. When you focus on what's not working, you're not functioning in your full creatorship, which keeps you from amplifying higher timelines to consistently work with. Most of the news you see is just a distraction that's controlled by a small number of media outlets. It's very one-sided and can't be trusted. By living love, your density awareness becomes higher, and your focus on matters involving ego, survival, and things like the car you drive becomes less. Accepting your creatorship is like gently traveling down a quiet river with ease and grace on an inner tube, knowing whatever you need, whenever you need it, you will create it.

56

Your genetic structure continuously mutates and adapts to whatever environment you're in. Science has shown that when sand is placed on top of a drum, the vibration of drumming creates patterns that look like mandalas. Your personal vibrational frequency seeks to be in harmony, so it uses similar patterns in your DNA to work with energies coming in or going out. Human genetics are wired to make wholeness happen to allow the process of renewal and integration. Things are going on all around us all of the time that we're not fully aware of because our focus is somewhere else, but when we change our focus to that of love we become like a wet sponge and try to absorb it all, especially things that resonate with our genetic blueprint. Because we are all creator beings, we can consciously speed up the changes going on within our DNA. Physical and spiritual evolution isn't about Darwin or God, it's about consciously shifting your internal focus and learning to transform your sluggish caterpillar human self into a beautiful divine butterfly.

57

Memories of Atlantis continue to haunt many high-frequency beings who believe what's happening now is the result of unresolved karmic issues from former Atlantean abuses of power, which is partially true, but lessons from other lifetimes are going on as well at the same time. The more aware you become of your multidimensional self, the more you realize that you've done this illusion before, been there, done that. However, you still have some polishing up to do on some of your rough edges before you're finally finished. It needs to be smoothed out a bit and for this reality to be experienced with a new perception, a different perspective, and an evolved understanding. You must heal this moment you're in right now, *not yesterday's moment*. For the Atlanteans of old, it was only about saving a continent, for us, it's about an entire planet.

58

Enlightenment feels like you're on a journey that encompasses all of your physical, mental, emotional, and spiritual aspects, requiring a total transformation, dying to all you've ever been and all you've ever believed to be true. Most of your beliefs were taught to you by someone you either admired, trusted, or feared and then accepted as your own, but they received it the very same way you did. What if the creator of that belief was mistaken? What if everything you believe was made up by someone with no idea what they were talking about? In Buddhism, students are given years of training to prepare for this sacred journey. Dr. Carl Jung said that as the layers of the ego are peeled away, all one finds at the end is an empty center … but enlightenment is not a journey into emptiness. It's a discovery of all the potential you were born with. Enlightenment is like staring into a full glass of clear water that only gives the appearance of being empty, and in that water can be found all your potential, to live love every day, to act consciously, to be focused, and to be in creatorship. You don't need to go on a journey to find it, you're already holding it in your hand, just drink it down, and enjoy it.

59

In 3-D, masculine and feminine are seen as separate, but in 4-D and 5-D, Divine Masculine and Divine Feminine are seen as just one energy working together in unity. The masculine and feminine energies found in 3-D are wounded and need to be healed, but society tends to glorify wounded behaviors with movies that promote violence. We must stop sending twisted messages about what the ideal masculine and feminine looks like, how a man should act, and a woman should be. We must be clear about masculine and feminine because when you're shifting back and forth between the positive and negative, it not only affects your behavior but also creates confusion about your ideal self. Consistency is needed because there are no masculine or feminine traits that are only masculine or all feminine. To be Divine, walls of separation disappear, they become a mixture of each other, and are often intertwined.

60

The stories in the news are very scary, it's like Halloween every day, saying the sky is falling, that famine, drought, and supply shortages are inevitable, that more sickness and disease are right around the corner, and that the future is very dark. These are reflections of your wounded masculine and feminine that need to be healed. They are in your life as a reminder of what's going on in your inner self. Negativity isn't where your focus should be. Lots of positive ideas are happening in the world. For example, plastic is being removed from the oceans, water is being drawn from the air, and clean fuel is being created from the methane emitted by global warming. Focus on the world you want to see rather than playing the victim card and believing all of the bad stuff we hear. This is a time of false prophets. It should be a time of Merlin and bring back magic to create the reality you want to live in. Like Halloween, you are just wearing a human costume. Beneath it lies the creator spirit you are. Reality is an illusion created by beliefs that can be changed. The worst thing anyone can do is to believe this illusion is real.

61

Your feminine and masculine are wounded. It's important to admit that because we can't fully shift out of the old 3-D paradigm and create a New World until we know what it is that needs to be changed in us. Your wounded masculine is at the heart of the problem with wars and racism at the top. Your wounded feminine doesn't believe she is strong enough to change. See your inner wounding, understand why it exists, face your traumas, and realize they built your thoughts, memories, and emotions, each of which holds a specific energy frequency. You must know what makes you angry and be able to feel your body reacting, but the same is true for what makes you happy and what you like about yourself. Feminine behavior is your inner workings, while masculine behavior is 'you' functioning in the world. Because the feminine lacks courage and feels not enough, it causes the masculine to abuse power and do destructive behaviors. Healing both the masculine and feminine requires making the leap into 4-D awareness by living love every day, because when you consciously change yourself, you change the world.

62

To 'wake up' is to be aware of your multidimensional aspects found in the higher frequencies. Activation involves consciously putting your Light into the world and being in service to help others wake up as well. Ascension involves you living love at your highest possible vibration. Creating a New World requires all three. We need awake, activated activists who are living love every day, but most humans have a bovine mentality which means they prefer to follow than lead, so when they make a mistake they just say, *oops,* then get back in line with the rest of the cattle, so to lead the herds, the world needs shepherds who have healed their wounded ego and are willing to learn from their mistakes, which requires getting beyond the cattle gates. Spiritual evolution is about 'You,' not 'Moo,' and allowing 'oops' to become 'ups' because doing so helps you grow. You are standing on the precipice for either creating a whole New World of awakened humans who are willing to stand up, be counted, and create new paradigms, or to remain in the old, content with being hooked up to multibillion-dollar corporate milking machines that continually drain their body, mind, and soul every day.

63

At times, everyone experiences fourth and fifth-density awareness, like when you're with your family on the beach while the sun is setting, the moon is rising, the seagulls are calling, and you're feeling the love. You gently slip out of this third-density experience and move to fourth. Holding a higher frequency vibration creates an expanded awareness of other dimensions, but when you get back home you must face the lower vibrations of an often-intimidating world, so then what happens? Do you fly off the handle, lose your temper, and go to a bar and drink? Practice 'living love every day' and consciously work at keeping your vibrational frequency high until it becomes the ordinary thing to do. That's when you can shift from lower fourth to upper fourth density. Once you've let go of all your internal crap and begin making the shift from 'living love every day' to 'love all, always,' love becomes more of a natural expression of the Spirit you already are, like a state of being rather than trying to make an effort to do or act. That's when you begin to experience fifth-density awareness almost all the time. Remember, Ascension is a process of expanding the love you are. It takes practice to go from our fear-based matrix to a world that is based solely on love.

64

What is the purpose of a sign? When the three wise men saw a huge star in the sky they knew it was a sign that something great was about to happen. In this New Age, something great is about to happen again. Is it going to take being hit over the head with a brick for you to see stars and to know it's time to wake up or to get blasted by a huge wave of cosmic energy from outer space to become Activated? The signs are everywhere. Waking up is to realize there is so much more to you than just a personality ego inhabiting a physical body. To be Activated is to get out of bed and create positive change. Living love every day isn't hard to do, but you must still do the inner work, identify what your core issues are, release your anger, your shame, and all of your fears ... and then replace them with something else that's much more loving.

65

It's imperative to realize that life on Earth is simply an experiment about *living love unconditionally at the highest vibration possible,* which means it's all right *to love everyone all the time*, no matter what. That's the Ascension process, to consciously expand our understanding of love from 3-D to 4-D to 5-D, and ultimately 6-D, from the outward feeling of separation to the knowingness of Oneness. However, other perspectives are also needed for an awakened person to survive in this third-density world. They must be in awe of the beauty and sensuality this planet has to offer, like believing in magic, accepting miracles, and having the willingness to fearlessly live their dreams. They must have the wisdom to know that with the Clear Light of Consciousness, and the Divine Light of Love all things are possible. When you leave your negativity behind, doorways open to a bright and positive future.

66

The energy of third density is reflective because it vibrates at such a low frequency, which allows physical form to be seen by human eyes. The higher frequencies are filled with beings who are called *the unseen,* Think of an airplane propeller, you can see it when it moves slowly but once it's moving fast it becomes invisible. Your vibrational frequency can be increased or decreased either consciously or unconsciously. Things like too much coffee, getting stressed out, or going for a jog can cause your heart to pump harder, but just because something makes your body speed up doesn't mean your vibration is getting any higher. You raise your vibrational frequency with things that allow your mind and body to slow down, like meditation, tai chi, yoga, going for walks in nature, eating healthy, or taking a hot bath. The best way to increase your vibrational frequency is to practice living love every day, which activates you. You feel better, happier, and have more awareness, and for some, the world that had been previously unseen becomes visible.

67

You are the Universe. It starts with you. Everything you perceive begins within your mind. It's at the very center of all your experiences. Astrophysicists and neuroscientists teamed up to compare similarities between the Universe and networks of neurons in the brain. Despite the substantial difference in scale, the two systems were strikingly alike. They used a combination of methods from cosmology, neuroscience, and network analysis to quantitatively compare the two and found that describing the human brain as a 3-pound Universe may be closer to the truth than we thought. The most complex and fascinating structures known to science are the human network of neurons in your brain and a nearly invisible web that connects galaxies throughout the cosmos. The resemblance is uncanny. The word UN-I-VERSE translates into, "I Am-One-Song." It means you have a unique vibrational frequency. The Bible says, *"in the beginning was the Word."* Instead, it should say, *"in the beginning, was the Song."* The earliest religious text is from India, the Bhagavad Gita, which means, *"Song of God."* It's your song; the song of your god within. When you release the illusion of this world by living love every day, basking in the higher vibrational frequencies, you hear the song loudly singing throughout the Universe that you are.

68

One of the hardest and most often asked questions is, *What is love?* Human love is third-density love. For many, it has to do with feeding your addictions and survival needs, things that have to do with the ego, like food, touching, money, health, feeling safe, or your codependency. But the energy of love transcends dimensions. The higher frequencies of love have little to do with the ego. Love can be defined as *expansion* because that's what love does. It's like a layer of doorways that allows your awareness of Consciousness to grow. Scientists have proven that the Universe is constantly expanding, *and that Universe is within you,* which means you're in a state of constant expansion. So ask yourself, *how fast do you want to expand*? That's what the Ascension Process is. It's about making a conscious choice to live love at the highest possible vibrational frequency and move far beyond the needs of the human ego.

69

Categorizing your daily experiences with your mind is what your brain does because of how you perceive time and space in third density, but when you're working in the higher densities you can see the bigger picture because you're higher up on the mountain and see much more. Your perspective is enlarged and everything about you, your gut, heart, and brain, all have a greater perception. In 3-D, you're like a horse with blinders so you put 'spiritually' into a box, believing that things affect you physically, mentally, emotionally, and spiritually, but it's not true. Everything you do, say, think, or believe should be considered spiritual. It should encompass your day and night, being in conscious awareness, appreciative, and grateful. As you move into 4-D and 5-D, perceptions of time and space merge as 3-D's reflective aspect begins to fade away. The same thing happens in the Death Realm after your brain function has stopped. Consciousness continues, but because there's no longer a physical brain to categorize experiences, your past thoughts, memories, beliefs, and emotions come together as one grand spiritual realization that eventually becomes wisdom. After your earthly ego function ends, that wisdom is what your Spirit takes with you into the next lifetime. The only question you will ask yourself is ... *did I love enough?*

70

You do not die, there is only transformation. The Afterlife is about returning to wholeness. Other than consciousness, everything is energy. This physical world is simply a stepped-down version of vibrational frequencies that are so slow they give the appearance of being solid. Einstein said, "energy is always conserved, it can neither be created nor destroyed, only be transformed." In other words, energy is recycled. When we leave this Earth, the same consciousness that created your earthly low-frequency body creates a higher-frequency energy body. When consciousness focuses on your earthly body we call it a Soul, but in other realms, we call it a Spirit. You are forever, always have been, and always will be. You've done this illusion hundreds of times before. There is no reason to fear death. You are always in a constant state of expansion, just like the Universe. The Ascension process never ends. You can return to Earth for another lifetime or choose to be part of an endless number of other experiments in other realms that are ready and waiting for the consciousness that you are to explore. In your journey throughout this Universe, you are both the scientist and the lab rat.

71

As I said previously, never fear death, but someday, the experiment called humanity must end. It would be a tragedy if the Akashic Records of galactic history showed that the human race destroyed itself during times of war, rather than being reabsorbed by the Universe during times of peace. Are you willing to lose this beautiful planet simply because of the egotistical whims of a few who want to have power over others or those who refuse to part with the wealth they stole from the sweat and blood of hard-working people? Throughout the world, everyone must learn to step up to the plate and knock the ball out of the park. That means holding everyone accountable and responsible for creating a sustainable future, especially those who run governments and control the wealth on this planet. Don't be a doormat or allow yourself to be prodded like cattle. Activate Activists are not jellyfish. Be willing to forgive the past. Never lose hope for humanity. Live love every day, never allow the illusion to push you to violence, but do remain fearless, strong, courageous, and impeccable. If we do nothing, we are nothing.

72

If nothing changes within the next ten years, if things remain the way they are now, stuck in a fear-based capitalistic consumer economy of third-density awareness with humans all competing for the same things to make their lives easier, then lifeforce energy on Earth will be in serious danger. This is a pivotal point regarding the fate of humanity. Everyone must get off this hamster wheel and begin creating massive change by using our creative Divine Feminine energy to come up with ideas and our Divine Masculine energy to put tone ideas into action. We can't depend on governments to fix this world. Billionaires and multi-million-dollar corporations must voluntarily use up to 30% of their wealth. They have the technology, the manpower, and the money. Together, they can restore oxygen to the oceans, remove polluted air from cities, feed masses of starving people, remove nuclear waste from the planet, and restore the ozone layer, *just to mention a few*. That way, they would no longer be seen as villains, but as heroes. Those without wealth must still do their fair share as well by putting in ample time to clean up and repair the environment they live in. For the creation of a New World to be successful with a sustainable future, it requires a joint effort of unity with love and compassion by everyone, not just a few.

73

For things to run smoothly, you must get rid of the obstacles holding you back. Time is of the essence. Only a few short years still remain to prepare for the challenges we are facing. The future requires letting go of the past and releasing feelings of anger, shame, and blame, but to do this effectively requires forgiveness and most people don't know how to successfully forgive. Four steps are needed. First, forgive anyone who offended you, even if they have died or can no longer be found. Second, forgive yourself for your role in what happened because there are always two sides to every story. Third, forgive your Soul and your Higher Self for having put you in that situation. Fourth, and the most important, is to forgive God. A lot of people are very angry at God. When a loved one dies, or if you become ill, God is first to be blamed. Even if you don't believe in God, forgive God anyway. Doing so fills in any gaps the first three steps didn't cover. Remember, forgiving the past doesn't mean what someone did was right, it just means that you're ready to move on and do what's needed to prevent it from reoccurring. We must learn to let go of our hurt from the past and forgive it. This is needed to create a whole New World based on love and compassion.

74

Gandhi drove the British out of India by following the principles of nonviolent civil disobedience. In the Sixties, the Hippies created the 'Peace & Love movement' to bring an end to the Vietnam War and the military draft. Both eventually ended, but the Hippies fell into disarray when radical factions called *Yippies* took violence into the streets by fighting the police. Today's youth face similar challenges because until lessons have been learned, history repeats itself. Today's generation also believes in peace and nonviolence, but many have pent-up anger, blaming the older generation for their problems, and react with violent behavior or refuse to take responsibility for the future, claiming the past wasn't their fault. For a New World to be successful, we must learn from the past, but also forgive the past, and then deal with the present. Hold fast to your convictions about peace and don't get sucked into the illusion of power. You can't be for peace and at war with others at the same time. Don't be against anything and retain your passion for peace despite how crazy the illusion seems to get. There is only *"one peace"* to the puzzle of how to end war. www.StoryofaHippie.com.

75

Hurt, anger, and sadness often weigh heavily upon our shoulders. Take the story of the man who carried a sack full of rocks on his back for several years. One day, he finally let go of it and felt 100% better, was lighter, and no longer in pain. That's what negative emotions do, but they are nothing more than a sack full of rocks. With forgiveness, you can let go of negativity anytime you want. Don't waste your life carrying things you don't need or no longer serve you. Forgiving the past allows you to grow and move forward. This is how we should deal with offenders of the law because everyone deserves a second chance. The Bible says, *turn the other cheek and do unto others as you would be done by.* Those who are dangerous to others or themselves should be separated from others until they're not, but incarceration has been proven to be ineffective in the reduction of crime. Instead, it destroys your Spirit, ruins your life, damages your family, and creates a burden on society. It's time to try something new, how about love? First-time, non-violent offenders of the law should always be offered reasonable alternatives to incarceration. We must all be more forgiving, loving, and compassionate, including victims. *www.TheCrystalTrilogy.com*

76

The quest for power is an illusion. It comes from an inner wounding that says, "*I am not enough, so I need to have more.*" On the other hand, self-empowerment is allowing ourselves to function as a positive force of Source energy in this world. Enlightened people trust the Universe to provide whatever they need by being available whenever it's needed. Have you found that kind of trust? Religious people often use 'faith' as their escape clause. Their beliefs in just about anything are based on 'faith in God,' but to take responsibility for your future, *faith in God* might not be the best choice. In the story of Noah, God allowed the world to be destroyed by a great flood. The Akashic Records say this world was destroyed on four other occasions. In other words, this is the fifth opportunity we've been given to get it right, this is our last chance. Creating a whole New World requires an attitude of self-empowerment that goes far beyond faith in God. You must love yourself completely and have trust in the Universe, hope for humanity, and faith in yourself.

77

People often ask, *what does it mean to 'completely' love yourself?* Loving yourself completely is to realize you are married to yourself. It's your human self and Spirit self quietly whispering to each other, "Until death do we part." It's the full recognition and surrender to your Divine Mother-Goddess within, who your human self loves more than any other thing or person in this world, It's to look into the mirror and proclaim, *I will no longer judge who I am or compare myself to others. The way that I am right now is absolutely perfect, for me.*

78

What does it mean to be Activated? It's a lot like being energized. When you're focused on your human self, it's called being motivated, but when you wake up to the fact that there is so much more to yourself than just being human, you begin to focus on your Spirit self and the love that you are. You feel the call to be of service, put wings on your love, and begin to fly. That's when you know you've been Activated.

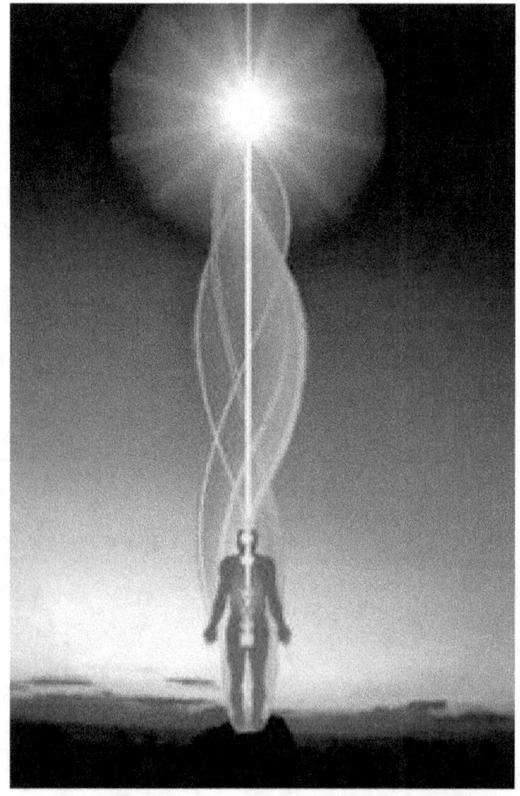

79

A young man once asked, "What's the difference between religion, spirituality, and science?" A wise old man answered, "Religion is for those who fear going to hell, spirituality is for those who have already been through hell, and science is for those who enjoy creating hell for the rest of us." Interestingly, several hundreds of years ago, religion and science were considered to be the same, until science finally broke free from the clutches of religious dogma. In the future, science will be able to prove how everything in the Universe works. Someday, science and religion will again merge, but this time, religion will be held in the clutches of science. Because spirituality is always in a constant state of expansion and always changing, by its very nature, it shall remain free from any sort of boxes, borders, or definitions that try to contain it.

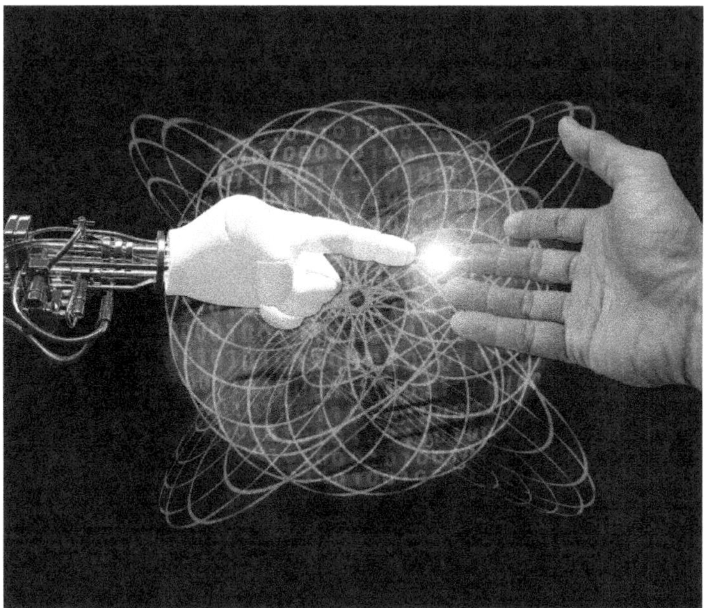

80

Do not believe all of the false prophets that you see on social media because almost everyone these days is telling us what the future holds. Everything is in a state of change because the Universe is constantly expanding faster than ever before, letting go of all that previously was, which is why it's also important to 'release the old' from your own life. No one can accurately predict exactly how future events will manifest. Energy can be molded, shaped, and sculpted into limitless numbers of potentials that show up in any number of ways, which is one of the reasons that energy exists in the first place, so that we, as creators, can play with it and mold it into whatever we want. All that anyone can do is see energy patterns and then attempt to forecast their probability based on what's already happening. Even the best psychics are only about seventy percent accurate, and once you've released your hold on the past, the future becomes unpredictable. This is the way we're going to build a whole New World, by releasing and forgiving the past, then allowing a previously unimaginable creation to become the new dream.

81

The caterpillar sluggishly moves across the ground, climbs up a tree, and builds a cocoon. As it first enters, it seems to be the end of its world, but when the butterfly emerges, it's the beginning of a whole new world and it flies off into a wide-open blue sky. The same idea applies to those who believe their world is only about pain, suffering, anger, frustration, separation, and isolation. They fear the transformation that the chrysalis offers because their ego is so full of negativity and judgments that their perceptional truth can't imagine letting go of the only experience they have ever known ... but when they allow themselves the transformation, a whole new existence begins as a whole new beautiful creature.

82

You must never believe the illusion is real, which is especially true regarding your ego, otherwise, you will get too comfortable with the old ways and lose this golden opportunity to create new paradigms for a whole New World. Your ego was created by 'you' between the ages of two and seven as a survival mechanism and is filled with all sorts of superstitious beliefs. The fact is, most of what you were taught about this reality just isn't true, so it's important to release beliefs that say your ego might be something real. It didn't exist before you were born and begins to fade away shortly after you die. Your ego is *who you are* only as your human experience, but *what you actually are* is your Spirit. Take some quiet time each morning 'to just be' … to just be still and explore your Universe within yourself, for that is your true inner nature.

83

Power is an illusion, but when people believe in power it allows fear into their lives, and real or not, power often has influence over others. For many, their need for power and control keeps them trapped like an animal in a human zoo because although it feels like freedom, in reality, it's a prison within your mind, a limitation of consciousness that I call, *The Crystal Prison*, but self-empowerment is not an illusion because you are choosing to be free of fear, and because all of your experiences come from within, you realize that external power can't exist. It's just a belief that's been woven into the mind of mass consciousness that came from all of the Old Testament stuff that taught us to fear God. Remember, there is nothing greater in the Universe than that which is already within you. Soon, the grip that power has over this world will be released and transformed. No longer will people be duped by those in powerful positions in both government and religious organizations. Power will be replaced with self-empowerment, which allows people to be who they are. This will be needed to create a whole New World.

84

There actually is a *Divine Plan* as well as a *Blueprint* for humanity. The Plan never changes but the Blueprint can adjust depending on what energies humanity has available to work with at the time. The Plan is the ultimate goal, the Blueprint is the means to get there. The Plan is for humanity to experience love at the highest possible vibration, and the means to achieve that goal is to live love every day, however, for the Plan to succeed, certain timelines must be met that are part of your spiritual evolution. Timelines are about letting go of your human stuff, things like worrying about the future, creating expectations, holding on to old beliefs about how things must be done, not allowing yourself to see other perspectives than your own, and not being willing to change your subconscious programming. Timelines are density shifts from this fear-based third-density experience to a fourth-density experience that is more love-based and compassionate. The fifth-density experience is called a Divine-human, often referred to as the 'Master' or the 'Merlin.' To the mind of others, things seem to appear like magic, but what the fifth-density experience does is allow energy to be in service to you.

85

It's time for humanity to change its perspective of how they view the process of dying and the end result, which we call death. Instead of being in fear and believing that the end of life is also the end of one's earthly ego and identity, we must realize that releasing one's ego is a positive thing and that the dying process allows you the opportunity to connect with your inner Spirit. Dying is not about losing one's identity or physical body, it's about allowing yourself the freedom to go on to something much more expressive and expansive than you could ever do in your human form. The dying process marks a new beginning that begins taking place long before physical death occurs, and once it does, your so-called 'death' is simply a gentle return to wholeness.

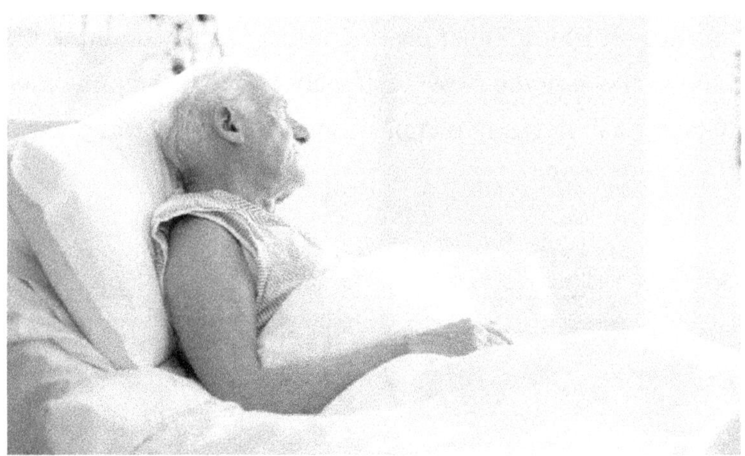

86

In America, the model for our fear-based criminal justice system was modeled after the Old Testament Biblical belief of the Afterlife. For example. the Offender, i.e., the Defendant, has been sitting in jail, has essentially died, and now sits in judgment. A Bar separates Heaven and Earth with a gate (the Pearly Gates) that is protected by a Bailiff or Sheriff who wears a star on his shirt like an angel. Once the Offender has been told what he is charged with, the Prosecutor's job is to prove the Offender is sinful. The Defender's job is to prove they are righteous. They stand in front of a Judge who represents an Angry God and wears an ominous long black robe who is to pass judgment and sentence the Offender but rarely offers forgiveness. For the more serious offenses, a Jury is chosen that represents an Angelic Choir sitting in a row of seats as if on a cloud singing out the verdict. If the Offender is found to be guilty, he is sent to Hell (prison) for punishment, but if found innocent, he returns to Earth for another chance at life. Don't you think it's time to start living the way the New Testament taught, which is based on a loving God who believes in compassion and turns the other cheek?

87

Angels practice Divine Neutrality and non-judgment so they don't get involved in human politics or even disputes between nations unless it involves the fate of the planet, but as a human…*what should you do?* On October 28, 2021, several large oil company executives admitted to Congress for the first time that global warming was real and confessed to having deceived the public for years because a former lobbyist had revealed documents proving it. But even with the admission of guilt, they would still not take responsibility by refusing to admit that the world was facing a crisis. Instead, they simply said we were facing a challenge and would not agree to lower carbon emissions. You might not be an angel yet, but you can be an Activated Activist here on Earth. Focus your energy on making the big oil companies change the current paradigm and consciously begin working towards healing the planet.

88

Everything we perceive as being outside of us has something to do with what's going on inside of us. *As above, so below* can also mean, *as on the outside, so on the inside,* because we create our own Universe. The energies used by our Consciousness for this earthly experience begin as Divinely Neutral, but as the creative gods we are, we assign labels and definitions to that energy at a very young age, which includes everything our senses encounter, which affects our knowledge, desires, and wisdom. The energy of all the other Souls around us becomes part of those definitions and labels, so we tend to perceive them as good, bad, happy, angry, or whatever. But we can change those definitions and labels any time we want to. Even better, when you can accept that everything you perceive is simply a part of what's going on with you and remain Divinely Neutral without assigning any labels at all, it will change everything as you begin to see the world for what it truly is, and others for who and what they truly are. The Universe you perceive is a choice. It's up to you to decide what kind of world you want to live in.

89

It's true that wounded people have trouble with relationships, but the truth is, everyone living in 3-D is wounded because that's the nature of the 3-D experience due to the feelings of separation from Source that we have since we are born, therefore, to have the wounding experience is a necessary step in our journey to achieving wholeness. For example, *one must know pain before one can realize what having no pain means*, but the 3-D experience teaches that you can only learn through pain, such as, *no pain no gain*, so you get stuck in a loop of thinking that pain is the only way to grow. When we consciously practice 'living love' every day we can experience 4-D and move into a state of expansion in which pain is no longer relevant because the higher you go in with your personal vibrational frequency the less you focus on your physical body or other mundane cares of the world. Related to that is trauma, which is often used as an excuse for being stuck. Trauma has to do with a past event and the degree of the trauma depends on how much focus you are giving it. What may be traumatic for you may not be traumatic for someone else. We can't change what happened in the past, but we can change how the past is perceived. The best way to deal with trauma is first, to realize that it got you to this moment, and second, change your focus to something loving to bring out your passion for a future event, such as getting excited about the creation of a whole New World.

90

Humanity has been stuck in 3-D awareness for over 12,000 thousand years which was about the time of the great cataclysm that involved Atlantis, but once you consciously arrive at 4-D awareness, most of you will move through it incredibly quickly because fourth density is only a brief layover before boarding the '5-D Express,' then you'll be on the way to experiencing a whole New World. The higher-density timelines will open gateways of choice this world has not had before in areas such as education, finance, government, and as the new caretakers of the Earth. It will bring change from a consumer-based economy where even the most remote tribes on the planet now drink Coca-Cola, to one more consciousness-based that includes equality and equity. But how far the shift goes will depend on the choices humanity makes right now. Our world is corrupt, and dishonesty exists at all levels, but it's falling apart, literally crumbling because people aren't willing to allow it to exist any longer. This must be an Age of Integrity because it's difficult for individuals to Ascend if they must deal with dishonest governments and corporations on a daily basis. As the next decade begins to unfold, if we keep our focus on the new, much of the old will quickly collapse.

91

Emotions are often a reaction to something from the past, whereas passion has to do with sensing the possible outcome of a future event. Passion comes from your senses, which are real, whereas reactions are often produced from hormones and therefore are not. Sexual desire is a reaction, it isn't real, but a passion for beauty and sensuality usually is. One can be passionate about love, but not lust, which is a fabricated reaction. Happiness is a basic human need, although joy is preferred. However, happiness can just be a reaction to something that has already passed, but when you feel passionate about the future it creates a sense of joy, which is what you should ultimately seek. The color of joy is bright red, like you see at Christmas time, whereas dark red is the color of anger. Joy releases anger and creates balance, thereby healing both your body and mind. The shape of joy is an outpouring of openness and radiance that gives off a burning illumination like a fire that is free of limitation. Finding joy is one of the keys to creating inner relaxation and reducing stress. Find something to be joyful about and bring some heated passion into your life. Don't settle for being occupied, satisfied, content, and happy … like a cow grazing in an open pasture. Instead, you can find your joy in the creation of a whole New World.

92

There is no singular truth within the illusion, even the belief that we are limited to just five senses. There are thousands of senses available for humans, such as the sense of joy, anger, fear, freedom, oneness, love, awareness, entitlement, lack, passion, frustration, overwhelm, and abundance, but most of our senses will never be used because we've never been told they exist … *money in a bank does you no good if you don't know you have it.* It's also an illusion to believe that humans are at the top of the food chain or to think that what you know about the world is all there is. The illusion exists because we would like to believe nothing changes. It's hard for humans to relate to change because they want the material world to be real instead of the Spiritual Realms, but what you call 'reality' is the actual illusion ... and because humans think in hierarchical and linear terms, they tend to believe the most important things must be at the top, and that all the rest is somewhere beneath it, which is how humanity tends to view God … but the Universe is not a pyramid scheme. There is nothing at the top because there is no top, there is only you, and you are the Universe. You are, *'All That Is.'*

93

The pineal gland controls how much light gets distributed through your body. It also stimulates the pituitary and works with your brain to maintain certain bodily functions. In addition, the pineal is what opens your body's natural ability to function in altered states of consciousness. You start your life with a clear crystalline-like pineal gland, but as you age, it tends to harden and become less transparent, but you can reverse that process with diet and meditation. The clearer your pineal gland is, the more in touch you can become with your Spiritual world. As your Spirit learns to function in harmony with your body, it allows higher frequencies of energy to spread throughout your entire physical form. The clearer your body is, the clearer your pineal is likely to be as well. Every cell in your body works with photonic energy derived from light, and you function best when all of your cells become filled with light. For the last several years, you've been constantly receiving downloads of energy codes that are meant to create change within your body, and your pineal gland has been helping to balance that energy and store it. It's important to keep your pineal gland as clear as possible because as your DNA begins to change over the coming years, your pineal gland will become the ultimate key to experiencing your Light Body.

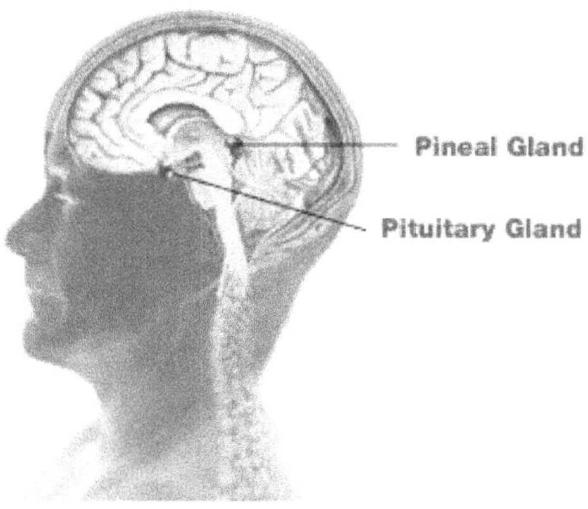

94

Having a healthy-functioning pineal gland is critical to increasing your spiritual vibrational frequency, your Light Body, and Ascension. Because the pineal converts light, it will play a key role when you're finally ready to consciously merge with your inner Light. The pineal tends to crystallize and calcify with age, but there are things you can do to prevent that. For example, some people use garlic and cucumbers for healing, but too much of it creates calcification…use them only in moderation, as well as onions, or any in the *alliaceous family* of plants. In fact, in the olden days, garlic and onions were only meant to be worn, not eaten, because the sulphone hydroxyl ion they contain gets into the brain and causes damage to the pineal. In cucumbers, cucurbitacin is found in the peel and seeds. Also, toxic chemicals such as fluoride, chlorine, and bromide, often found in drinking water, toothpaste, and cleaning products, accelerate crystallization. To reverse the damage to the pineal gland caused by these chemicals, try using 'green clean' products, drink distilled water, and always use fluoride-free toothpaste. Remove chemical-based products from your diet, including alcohol, because the pineal functions best when a constant flow of high spiritual energy is maintained, and for many, alcohol can act as a depressant. Furthermore, try to avoid the overuse of caffeine and other stimulants. The roasting process in coffee creates carcinogens in the beans, plus, anything that artificially stresses the body can calcify the pineal gland, which makes it unable to transform light in the way it's supposed to. For more information try reading my very unique and spiritual book,

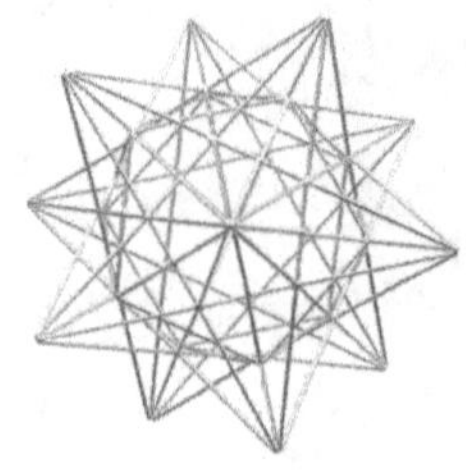

95

There are lots of things you can do to help decalcify your pineal, like sipping raw unfiltered apple cider vinegar throughout the day…just a spoonful in a glass of distilled water, perhaps with a touch of honey or malic acid, a natural organic sweetener found in fruits. In addition, begin eating a vegan diet. Animal products do not raise your spiritual vibration and put stress on your body, which can calcify your pineal and harden your arteries! A good vegan diet lowers your blood pressure and cholesterol. Humans and animals vibrate at a similar vibration, but plants exist in a whole different kingdom, have a higher frequency, and don't feel pain the same as animals do. With butchered animals, you run the risk of absorbing 'death hormones' generated at the moment it's killed. If it was farmed, you ingest the chemicals the animal is fed and treated with…plus, you absorb the animal's stress of living as a food producer rather than free roaming. The longer you're on a vegan diet, the more your respect for all forms of life increases, and compassion for the entire world. If you can, eat organic food. This may not always be possible, but unless it's organically grown, pesticides may have been used to preserve them for transport to market or filled with fertilizers absorbed during their growth, or subject to genetic modification, which can also be harmful to how your pineal gland functions.

96

Dreaming helps to keep the pineal gland functioning. If you have trouble dreaming, try melatonin or tryptophan before going to sleep. They contain melanin, a chemical that pigments our skin and has a lot to do with keeping the pineal healthy. People with brown and black skin generally have a clearer pineal than white-skinned people and their pineal tends to be bigger, which means they process the coding of light and utilize energy more naturally without the need to focus so much to make it happen, which allows for more receptivity of cosmic energy by having a better internal visual apparatus. They also dream, hallucinate, and meditate more vividly because their ability to translate light is stronger. But melanin is found in all human bodies, especially in your gut-brain, which deals with security issues. Melanin is built into the neuropathways, but because those of color have more of it, their pineal is less likely to occlude. Over the centuries, this knowledge has been covered up, neglected, and ignored but the ability to better connect with the Spirit World afforded to those with dark skin is still there due to the extra melanin. Having dark skin is a strength, not a distraction, and should never be considered a bad thing, but rather, a great gift.

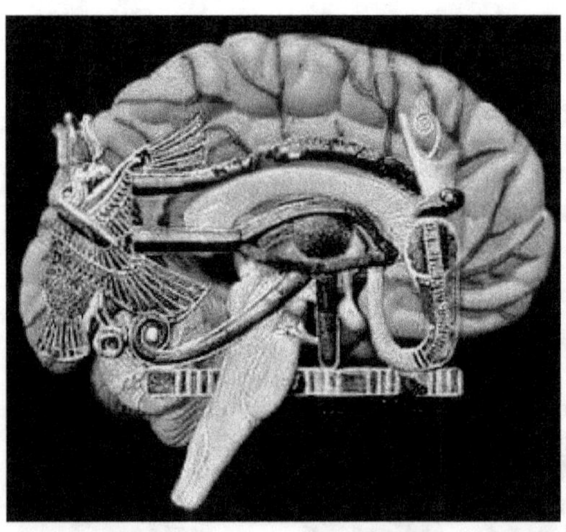

97

Your pineal gland can be cleared with meditation and visualization. For example, see your pineal gland as a small seed right behind your forehead, like a third eye, and imagine it spinning to the left and then to the right. You may feel your forehead tensing a bit, but that's to be expected, and the more you practice this exercise the faster it will spin and the less tension you will experience. Try doing this visualization while listening to a 480 Hz tuning fork or chime. Imagine a healthy, whole pineal gland in the front of your head, and imagine a beam of white Light coming towards you from the center of the Universe into your head and straight into your pineal gland, then filling your whole body with the white Light of love, enlightenment, and joy. Relax, let it be healing, and ask it to renew every cell and allow you to function at your very highest. Affirm that your pineal gland is functioning well, doing its job to serve you and this world. Offer gratitude at the end of the visualization. The pineal occasionally needs to rest, but because it's so sensitive to *any form of light*, it remains active unless it's in total darkness, therefore, we suggest that when you sleep, keep the room as dark as possible, cover illuminated devices and allow the pineal to take a couple of hours off from activity. Everyone needs a clear pineal gland with strong neuropathways to feel connected to the Universe while still in their body. A healthy pineal allows your body to function at a higher frequency beyond what can be seen within the normal energy spectrum of Light, which is needed to transform into a new Divine Human.

98

Realize that this world is all here for you, all the elements, of fire, wind, water, and earth. All the energies of your magnificent Universe are yours to play with. They are portals you can open. On the other side of these mysterious doorways are where the magic lies. Remember that you came here to be a Merlin magician, whose job is to bring back the magic to this planet. This is important because without believing in the possibility of magic there can be no hope. Right now, humanity needs to have more hope. Have trust in the Universe, faith in yourself, and hope for the world. Hope is what has always kept humanity going, for without it, there would only be hopelessness. Always be thankful and express gratitude. Gratitude tells the Universe you are ready for more, and without it, there would only be mass depression. That's the beauty of being a magician, for beyond these thresholds of hope and gratitude is where fifth density will be found, where emergence with your true self takes place, and where you can accept the depth of unlimited and unfathomable potentials to be made real and experienced here on Earth.

99

The only truth you should ever have…and your primary objective, is to know that you are a function of the Source Field who has come to this world to expand love by living love every day. The physical world you experience is a holographic image of how your subconscious mind senses energy. You are here to experience all of the energies this world has to offer but you must realize that you are not the experience, you are simply watching it as the experiencer. You are not sad, depressed, angry, sick, or lost, although at times you might internally feel that way. What you truly are is a whole, powerful, and beautiful spark of love that comes from the Heart of Source as a Pure Light of Consciousness. In the previous age, the Piscean Age, we discovered the Light that was already within us. In this age, the Aquarian Age, we're discovering how to put that Light into the world. Try to see yourself as a great being of Light, a function of Source in this world who has the confidence to overcome any challenge or obstacle that shows up, one who is flexible, purposely living love, and is not reactive but heart-driven. Greater is that which is within you than anything you perceive in the world, for everything you perceive is but a mirror, a reflection of your own beliefs.

100

Many times we talk about mystical events that create portals or doorways that create change. For example, someone might say that a solar eclipse opens a portal that will cause something big to happen in the future. The truth is, celestial and other mysterious happenings are not the portal itself. Rather, it is the energy of the event that opens something within you that helps you to remember what you truly are. That is to say, *you're the portal. It's you who is the doorway that opens.* Furthermore, you don't need to have some perplexing experience take place in your life to create that opening. What you already are lies at the center of your Universe. Everything you experience in this world is revolving around you … you do not revolve around it, so the easiest way to create what you want in your life is to allow it to come to you. As you begin to remember the Light that you are there will never be any need to chase after anything ever again! Stop, be still, and just be, and allow whatever it is you are looking for to find you … it will!

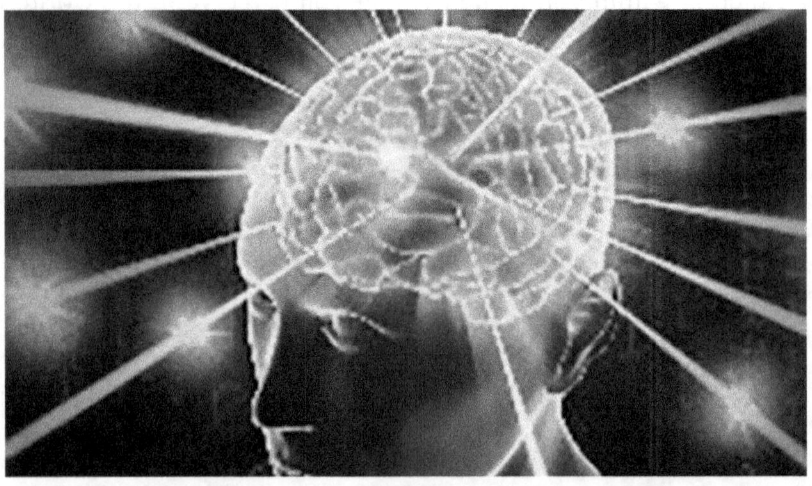

101 ... (101 to 120 are about Elementals and Angels)

Most of the planets in outer space are dead, not alive, although some form of life may still be found on them such as bacteria and viruses, but Earth has a soul much like humans, called Gaya, which maintains the Earth's functions and lifeforce energy. In the early days of creation, Gaya created helpers, workers, and protectors to assist with the basic elements of fire, water, air, and earth called *Elementals*. The reason you don't see them is because of the way humans have related to just about everything living on the planet, which is to say, they either kill them or ignore them. Elementals belong to what we call *the Devic Kingdom*, which lies in a nearby dimension that is still within the energy of the Earth Realm along with the Mineral, Plant, and Animal Kingdoms, but as 'created energy beings' under the direction of Gaya, their job is to assist all of those other kingdoms. Elementals that work with minerals, plants, and wild animals are called *Nature Spirits*, but those that assist humans and domesticated animals are called *Angels*. The word *Devi* comes from Sanskrit and means, *Shining Ones,* to describe their bright etheric form. When they do their jobs, Elementals come into physical form temporarily, which is when some people can actually see them.

102

The Earth Realm was first seeded by great Beings of Light causing the various planes and dimensions to be formed. The Devic Kingdom was created to assist in maintaining the planet's vital functions, just as you would do for your own body, or if you had a swimming pool and needed someone to come over once a week to take care of it. Because they are partially etheric, Devic creatures go back and forth between this third dimension and their dimension. Although they can intervene to give whatever assistance is necessary, they generally shy away from humans until they feel safe because humanity has been destroying their world for centuries. They help things grow, create rivers and lakes, help build mountains, purify the air, and clean the Earth with rain, all of which affect weather patterns, so many times, scientists are not able to accurately predict the weather when there is a lot of Elemental activity. With practice, you can call upon these weather fairies to give you the weather you want. Just give them a couple of days' notice and then put out your intention to have a nice day to go to the beach or to take a hike in the mountains. You'll be surprised at how often it works.

103

Nature Spirits, Elementals, or whatever name they are called has come from legend and folklore. In Celtic tradition, those assigned to work with earth are called Gnomes. Those that work with water are Undines. Those that work with air are Sylphs, and those that work to maintain the temperature for life to exist are Salamanders. In addition to Irish and Scottish folklore, many other names come from a variety of fairytales and are often interchanged, such as leprechauns, fairies, the wee people, pixies, brownies, trolls, etc., but the name I like best is 'Shining Ones.' To me, it's the most beautiful depiction of what they look like. The human visually experiences the sight of some of these workers while in their etheric form, but only from the corner of your eye as a bright speck of light or a shiny reflective surface, then quickly vanishes, which they do when you're looking at them. But do they look like Tinker Bell and have wings? No, they do not ... and of course, there is nothing to fear. In fact, once they know you mean them no harm they might try to play with you. For example, the wind could pick up very quickly and blow your hair on what seemed to be a normally calm day.

104

The mind is such that in the early stages of development primitive humans needed to see much more than is now necessary as a means of survival. Thousands of years ago they could see Elementals and angels much more clearly than we do now, although many children under the age of five still do. We lost our ability to see Elementals because as the mind developed, humans learned to take care of their basic survival needs, although at a subconscious level, they knew these beings were not going to harm them, therefore, they no longer needed to be aware of them, Even though we have long since tuned them out, with practice, you can regain that vision, but it's more of a clairvoyant than sensory, meaning it's not so much with your physical eyes but is the working together of several senses that finally allow you to say, *I can see them.* It's similar to the way you see the wind. You hear it whistling, you feel it blowing, observe branches moving, and leaves falling. Although you don't see the wind, you still can draw a picture of it. That's also the way you feel the presence of other energies. If you take the time to learn how to feel and see energy, you'll be able to recognize the light of the Shining Ones. At first, all you see is a flicker in the corner of your eye and say, *hey, what is that?* As you become more aware, you'll tune into things that have always existed but hadn't recognized before.

105

Elementals that help to maintain the chemical composition of the Earth are often found in caves. Those that work with plants often hide inside the knot of a tree. A friend once told me about a rather grouchy gnome who lived inside an old oak tree along a path where she walks her dog every morning. What do gnomes look like? Are they small, ugly, and green? Because they are etheric, elementals take on any form you project at them. Elementals look like whatever you think they do. First, you feel their energy, then your mind creates an image of what you've been told they look like. Granted, some Elementals can come into physical form temporarily but usually appear as a globe of light that looks somewhat like a candle flame with projections of light that look like wings to the human eye. When you get excited or energized, your auric field looks a lot like wings as well, plus you have a halo around your head. The light from an elemental may display a variety of different colors. The home of any Elemental is in a realm that's near wherever it is working at the time or providing service to a particular group of plants, minerals, or animals. Its home will be there because that's where it has been assigned to serve. If you are skeptical about the existence of gnomes, pixies, elves, leprechauns, ogres, trolls, sprites, or brownies, then ask yourself this, *do you think that people have been telling fairy tales for thousands of years for no good reason at all?*

106

Once Elementals become familiar with your energy and feel safe in your presence they may try to communicate with you, which they do telepathically by sending a seed thought into your mind. It's as though an entire communication appears inside your brain as a picture, instead of hearing a discussion. The original Chinese language was written like that so that one symbol would represent an entire thought. Elementals and angels work with you much like you do with domesticated animals by receiving images of what they are saying. You can also send them seed thoughts back in return but be as clear as you can with as much detail as possible about what you want them to do. A major element to communicating with Elementals, angels, and animals is to be able to discern the difference between your thoughts and the messages coming into your brain. This requires a very good understanding of your energy and how your mind generally functions. Much like a dog, elementals and angels love to be of assistance to humans and do it much more effectively when they can communicate directly with you.

107

Your Higher Self has a unique feel. Your Soul and Entity have yet another type of feel. When you speak with your Soul it feels like you're talking to God. Plus, there are even more aspects that make up your multidimensional self you're not yet in contact with. As you get to know what these others feel like, you can begin communicating with Elementals and Angels as well. Your thoughts are extremely powerful. It's the mind of mass consciousness that creates the consensus reality. Every thought you have becomes solid and manifests somewhere in some dimension. They don't always show up in this third dimension but will show up somewhere. Have you ever had a really good idea, and a month later it's in the news? Once you create it, it's out there, available for someone else to discover it, perhaps they see it in a dream. The clearer your thoughts are, the more solid they become. The clarity and intensity depend upon your ability to put yourself into the thought. Can you feel it, taste it, and smell it, and how well can you visualize it? Can you send your thoughts to someone else? Talking to Devic Beings is a lot like how you talk to your dogs and cats. If you have a pet, you probably talk to it all the time. The animal knows what you're saying and wonders why it is that you don't understand them. So, if you want Elementals to be present in your life, when you do your calling, also send an image of them appearing in front of you using your mind, and then be on the lookout, because if you allow it, they will show up,

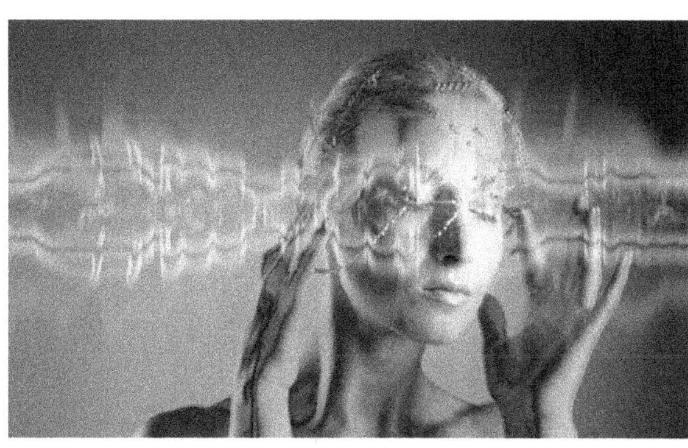

108

Once you learn to communicate with elementals, the word is going to spread, and soon, you'll become very popular, which is a good thing. Elementals are generally afraid of humans because over the centuries we have made things very difficult for them. We have cleared out their homes, mowed down their fields, and most of us don't believe in them. Fortunately, they are very forgiving, a bit like dogs! Here's a secret I'd like to share. The so-called Bigfoot, Sasquatch, and Yeti are nothing more than very big Brownies. They are Devic Beings that live in their own dimension of the Earth Realm but come into this third dimension to do their work as caretakers of the forests by using the shift in energy found in the Earth's ley lines. Native Americans recognized these large hairy creatures as Earth protectors They are found all over the world. They do not kill and are harmless so long as you don't attack them, but if they feel threatened, they will growl or even throw stones at you to try and scare you away. If you try to track them, they will run to the nearest ley line and seem to suddenly disappear without a trace, but in reality, they're just returning to their own dimensional realm for safety. That's why the chances of a Bigfoot being captured may never happen.

109

Water Elementals are called Undines in Celtic lore. They also work with sound because of its flowing quality. When you have difficulty with communication, ask the Undines to charge a glass of water and then drink it to get your voice back. Undines are among the brightest of the elementals and are often seen as sparkles playing on the water. Fire Elementals are called Salamanders. The name has nothing to do with lizards, although the idea of dragons does relate to transformation. Salamanders work with keeping the Earth at just the right temperature so life can grow. Fire transmutes, purifies, and strengthens. If you're catching a cold, call upon them to give you protection. Air Elementals are called Sylphs. When you first learn to work with elementals they're the easiest to work with and are often the first to come out and play with you in the form of wind. They enjoy working alongside Undines, so you often see wind and rain together. Air purifies and heals, which is why it invigorates you. A cleansing air bath in the nude allows your body to be surrounded by Sylphs. Sleeping outdoors or with a window open will help your body heal faster after an injury. Earth Elementals are referred to as Gnomes, but also include names like Leprechauns, Ogres, Trolls, and Brownies, and work with minerals, plants and trees. You can call upon them to help you find healing herbs and crystals. Native Americans often created a Medicine Wheel for healing that used the energy of all four elementals. Think of elementals as allies that are here to be of service to you. The ways they can be of help are endless.

110

Elementals are created energy beings whose purpose is to assist Gaya with assimilation, excretion, and processing the lifeforce they've been assigned to work with, just as humans process what they need and release what's no longer needed, like carbon dioxide. But you can also call upon elemental energy for personal assistance. For example, if you want tomorrow to be nice for hiking, call upon the ones who work with the climate, or as I call them, Weather Fairies. The more advance notice you give, the more likely a calling will work. When I say calling, that's exactly what you do. You call out to them, "I call upon the Undines, Sylphs, and Salamanders for a sunny day tomorrow." If this is your first time working with Nature Spirits and they don't know you, remember, they tend to be fearful of human energy because you're a very powerful being, and what humanity has done over the centuries has created a lot of pain and havoc for them. Don't extend your energy outward and yell, "Come here!" If it's too strong they won't respond, so consciously pull your energy in and gently say, "I call upon you for your assistance." Pulling your energy inward says you desire that no harm come to them, but even then, it may take several tries because they're shy. Over time, they will come out and play whenever you put out the call, and you'll develop a better sense of what they're saying to you. If you feel their presence, give thanks to them for being there. Then they'll interact with you much more often and even tell their friends about you.

111

Elementals have taken care of our planet since the days of creation. Some people offer gifts of food to the 'wee people.' They don't eat it, but the offering thanks them for sustaining Earth. The Devic Kingdom exists because of Gaia, the soul of our planet. She is why Earth is alive. In a hierarchical diagram of the Devic Kingdom, Gnomes are the most basic, then Undines, Sylphs, and Salamanders. After Nature Spirits are Angels and Archangels. At the very top would be the Spirit of Gaia, who uses Elementals 'for the Earth' and Angels 'for those on Earth.' Neither ever evolves into a human because they are not soul beings but are created beings. The reason why knowing about Nature Spirits is important is because Gaia will be leaving, but do not worry, it will take hundreds of years. As Earth's functions begin to unravel because of her departure, humanity will learn to take over. It is already happening, such as cloud seeding to deflect the sun's rays and to prevent warming. Very soon, humans will become the new caretakers of Earth, and will completely replace the role of Nature Spirits, which is part of the Plan, *to create a New Earth*. Now, I'm going to leave the world of Elementals behind and have a discussion about Angels. Most of what you read will not be found anywhere but here, or in the numerous books I've written about some of the lost and sacred wisdom needed for our world.

112

Angels have one primary purpose, to serve Earth's lifeforce energy. Angelic energy is different than Elemental energy. It is Novic Energy, associated with Super Novas which has also been called Ellic Energy. As a result, our ancestors referred to Angels as 'the Els,' with names like Micha-el, Gabri-el, Rapha-el, and Uri-el. Angels assist animals and humans as they move through the various realms of the wheel of life, such as the Birthing Realm, the Earth Realm, and the Near Realm of death. As a very general statement, lesser angels work with animals, Archangels work with humans, and at times with domesticated animals closely tied to the fate of a human, such as a rescue or service animal. Like Elementals, Angels generally appear in the form of light. They do not have wings, but their glow often looks like wings. They can briefly take on human form as an angel unaware. Someone pops into your life very briefly to assist you, and then they're gone and never seen again, causing you to wonder if they were real or not. As a created energy being, an Angel will not do anything to harm a human, they are strictly here to help. Much like Elementals, you can learn to call on them to be of assistance to you whenever you want so long as the intent of your request is for the highest good and is not based on your negative ego.

113

Do you have a Guardian Angel? The answer is both, 'yes and no.' Anytime you need assistance, you can call upon Angels for help, but they are not assigned to you as so many people believe. There's a lot of misinformation and confusion about Angels. There are two different kinds of Angels, those THAT BE, and those THAT DO. The Angels THAT BE are the Seraphim. They are the ones most would call 'good' because they are passive. They encompass Earth with vibrations of love and healing and assist humans during their journey from the time of their death until they are ready for their next incarnation. The Angels THAT DO are the Cherubim, often referred to as Cherubs, who many think of as Cupid, but they also include the ones we call Archangels. Over the centuries the Cherubim have been considered 'havoc workers' because they interact with humans while they're alive. As a result, you have one group of Angels who are viewed as very good and holy, and another that affects humanity's growth. Some people don't like being pushed like that, but their purpose is to get you through the lessons you would otherwise resist. The Seraphim are the ones that touch deep into your spiritual essence, and the Cherubim help you rise to the occasion.

114

When you think of Angels do you also think of demons? On Earth, there are only Angels and humans. Demons don't exist, and Angels are incapable of being harmful. The fact is, humans are the most dangerous form of life in the Universe. Angels are created beings that don't have free will the same way humans do, so no one can compel an Angel to do something that harms humanity. They are only here to help, but most humans don't like change, so their assistance often gets misinterpreted. Because of their manipulative ways, throughout the ages, the Angels THAT DO have been accused of many negative stories about change, choice, and possibilities, which has kept them separate from the Angels THAT BE. Those THAT DO create the friction required for human growth, to help you know what you're about, and to be a better person. Those THAT BE help with your spiritual connection to the Universe. The Seraphim represents Divine Feminine Energy, and the Cherubim represents Diving Masculine Energy. Together, their job is to enhance your spiritual growth, which they do, both on and off the Earth.

115

The Seraphim not only works with humans after death but constantly assists with everything on the Earth by emitting a divine radiance, much like a sacred song that surrounds the planet. The Cherubim work with humans during their lives and are usually referred to as Archangels. What image comes to mind when you think of a Cherub, a pudgy child with wings and no neck, shooting arrows to make humans fall in love? Cupid is just one example of how the Cherubim, those THAT DO, have been portrayed by humans for centuries, but the Archangels are thought of as powerful. The Cherubin have been called upon for ages to do all sorts of things. Gabriel is said to have visited Mary, the mother of Jesus, and the prophet Mohammad in their dreams. Most people have only heard of a few Archangels, like Rafael, Michael, Gabriel, and Uriel, but hundreds more exist. Traditionally, Rafael helps with new beginnings. Michael helps with manifestation. Gabriel helps create gentle endings, to overcome obstacles, and to heal. Uriel helps you face the unknown. Calling upon Archangels for help is similar to calling upon Elementals. It takes a lot of practice, but first, you must believe they actually exist, otherwise, when they show up after you call them, you won't recognize the shift in the energy, you won't feel their presence, and chances are, you won't be able to hear them when they speak back to you.

116

Humans don't have much contact with the Seraphim while they are alive, but they'll be there for you in the Afterlife. They also like to sing sacred tones that resonate around the planet to create a sense of peace, harmony, and tranquility, which can be felt when you are out in nature and far away from the hustle and bustle of the cities. When photographs are taken of the Earth from deep outer space, you can see the presence of the Seraphim, which shows up as a small ring of light surrounding the planet. When calling the Cherubim, first, create a sacred space. Next, ask for assistance, give thanks, and release them. If you ask these shining beings if they are Michael or Gabriel they're likely to say what you want to hear. They are here to be of service and will be whoever you want. If you say, *who are you,* they might not reply because energy does not have names like humans. The ones we call them were given by the Church. Their real names are made up of geometric sounds, and when said in the proper cadence can invoke powerful energies that can affect physical matter. Our ancestors called this 'Angel Magic.'

117

Energy exists to be in service to Consciousness. Ancient Egyptians were well-known for their use of magic, particularly, Angel Magic. They also knew there was no such thing as good magic or bad magic because energy is neutral. They would use the energy of angelic names to create thought forms to guard the entrance to pyramids. During the Dark Ages, in Europe, the names of Angels were used to create what the Church called *magical spells,* used to heal the sick from the plague. Angels are here to serve humanity. Their energy cannot be used for evil intent, but out of jealousy and ignorance, those within the Church who lived in fear called it black magic and accused the healers of witchcraft, claiming they were aligned with the Devil, even though Jesus often used Angel magic to heal people and to perform his other miracles. Angelic energy releases great power, and humans tend to abuse power, so in ancient times, the names of Archangels were kept hidden from the public and were instead written down using a secret code on metal, or on stone seals called amulets and talismans. The names written on the seals could not be used by anyone untrained or uninitiated so muggles would wear the amulets around their necks for protection, believing they would be kept free from psychic attack or physical harm.

118

Is it possible for a human to become an Angel or an Angel to become a human? No, a human is a Soul-Being with a physical form who has an innate ability to realize its connection to Source. An Angel is an energy being with an etheric form that is here to assist humanity with its spiritual evolution, but Angels can take on the illusion of a human for a brief period to give assistance, relay an important message, or do what is needed at the moment. An Angel can come into your life that looks human, *temporarily*. It's also possible for a deceased friend or relative to watch over you as an Angel and some entities that are not angels may seem like one. Likewise, there are humans (like shamans) who are often mistaken for angels because they can enter the spirit world and work directly with the deceased. But will an Angel save your life by suddenly appearing out of nowhere and keep you from falling? It depends upon the situation. Everything happens for some reason. Sometimes an injury or accident happens because you were clumsy or not thinking, but many 'accidents' happen to teach you a life lesson or were built into your karmic blueprint. Angels are here to assist but are not here to interfere with free will, karma, or what is meant to happen, so they might or might not intervene. Angels are eager to get involved in whatever way they can, especially with your spiritual growth.

119

Gaia will be leaving in a few hundred years but by then humanity will have learned to take over the function of Elementals. This will also be true for Angels. As humanity moves into fifth-density awareness, negativity no longer exists so there will be no need for the Cherubim to assist you with your spiritual growth. For a whole New World to come into being, even the Afterlife must change. As you learn to master your Light Body, the Near Realm will no longer be the transition point where the human ego is shed because it will already be gone. The role of the Seraphim as your guides during your Afterlife experience will not be necessary, nor will their role in sending peaceful vibrations to surround the planet. Once you identify more with a Light Body instead of a body of carbon, you will be half-human and half-angel, a whole new species of human living on Earth whose DNA is designed to survive the future and eventually expand to the farthest corners of the Universe.

120

The Biblical version of Michael says he is good, and Lucifer is bad. After God created Earth a battle took place. Lucifer means *Light Bearer or Morning Star* and had been God's best friend, but because of envy, pride, and desire, Lucifer rebelled and convinced a third of the Angels to join him. Michael remained loyal and defeated Lucifer, then cast him to Earth to become known as Satan, meaning *adversary*. His supporters were also cast out and called demons. The Cult of Michael is very old. Its followers worship Michael as *God's heavenly warrior* who fights battles in the name of God, as most wars are. Michael appears in the Hebrew Kabbala, mystical drawings of the Assyrians and Hittites, and in the holy books of Christians and Muslims. Michael means *like God* and is associated with the Sun, depicted with blonde hair, a bright halo, and holding a flaming sword. *Now, there's another version that says*: the Earth was created as a place where Spirits volunteered to experience the sensuality of third density, but feelings of separation existed, as well as negative emotions and ego, so it was easy to get stuck in the illusion. Angels were created to help humans get through this, and Lucifer was the best, a Bearer of Light from the primary source of creation energy coming to Earth, which was Venus. He was the first to be of service and chose to leave, but Michael stayed, feeling that humans were much too wild and dangerous. Over time, Lucifer fell prey to the illusion of human emotions like envy, pride, and desire, which don't exist in the higher realms, so Michael would not allow Lucifer to return until he'd worked through all of his negative stuff. Lucifer had no choice but to stay and help humanity change, which gave him a very bad reputation because humans hate change. So Michael became the head Archangel. Angels exist to help humans, but they know not to get too close because like Lucifer, humans can only access the higher realms after they shed their ego, release their negative emotions, and live love every day.

121

Everything you do is based on everything you see and judge, so what you move towards is based on how successful it was in the past. But if it's a brand-new thing, like jumping out of an airplane to skydive, your brain relates to what you think the experience will be like based on experiences you've already had. You think it will be like jumping off of a 10-foot wall, or like air blowing on your face while driving, or the time your stomach turned, and you felt nervous. Anything the brain can relate to will tell you what to expect. The problem is that you do not get the experience 'as it is.' You get it as you want it to be, which leads to disappointment if it's not what you expected, but then you just pat yourself on the back and say, *I knew it would be like that.* But anytime "this is what I thought it would be" shows up, it means that you're not getting it. Anytime you think you've got it ... it means there's something you're missing. You will always be a student, you are always learning, life is a process, and you never master anything fully. If you think you have, then you didn't do it right. Never be content with life. Change is constantly happening, otherwise, you're in a state usually called, *Dead.* Get into the frame of mind for creating a New World just as Cat Stevens sang in his famous song, Peace Train, *"Now come and join the living, it's not so far from you, and it's getting nearer, soon it will all be true."*

122

Forgiveness brings an end to karma. The Church says everyone is born into sin but sitting in judgment is more of a human thing rather than that of Spirit, so if you sin against society, low-frequency humans want to sentence you to prison, pay restitution, do community service, or be on probation, leaving you with the stigma of a convicted felon. We are not born into sin, but we do come here feeling separated from Source, which may feel like some sort of sin. Fortunately, humanity's awareness of Consciousness has evolved somewhat but is still a long way off from applying unconditional love to living our everyday lives. The only thing punishment does is to create even more separation and divisiveness, and therefore, more suffering. It's time to tear down the walls of the old beliefs that no longer serve us, including the fear-based paradigm of retribution, and create a new one that no longer follows the ancient system of payback. For a whole New World to be created, all of our institutions, including the criminal justice system, must be built with new foundations composed of loving Divine Feminine intent combined with compassionate Divine Masculine action. The only sin that exists is to just sit back, watch, and do nothing to change it.

123

Change requires revolution, but it must be peaceful, so what we want is a consciousness revolution. What may seem like chaos is actually an opportunity to create something new. Chaos is what we are seeing right now as masses of people are demanding change. After things fall apart will come a time to rebuild, so if you want to live in a whole New World don't create the same thing you had before. A new Earth is not about reform, it's about creating something entirely different. To see change, first, see it in yourself by doing something outrageous. That's what gets attention, but building a New World needs planning, vision, organizing, sharing, and cooperation from those who are conscious and awakened. What you build must be strong, not temporary, or else it will go back to the old way it was before. Start by providing a cushion of loving intent and create with compassion. A good place to begin would be with an equitable economy based on long-term sustainability. When energy is changing, if you add love to the equation, it's easier to let go of the old fear-based paradigm. Remember, you can never let go of or release anything permanently until it has been replaced with something else. Almost all of our major paradigms are crumbling. Removing what is fearful and inserting love-based intent with compassionate action will create a new way of doing things, but to make it last we must act in unity to create the foundations that are needed and then allow these new paradigms to become priority functions throughout our world.

$$(y - 0.75\,|x|)^2 + (0.75\,x)^2 = 1$$

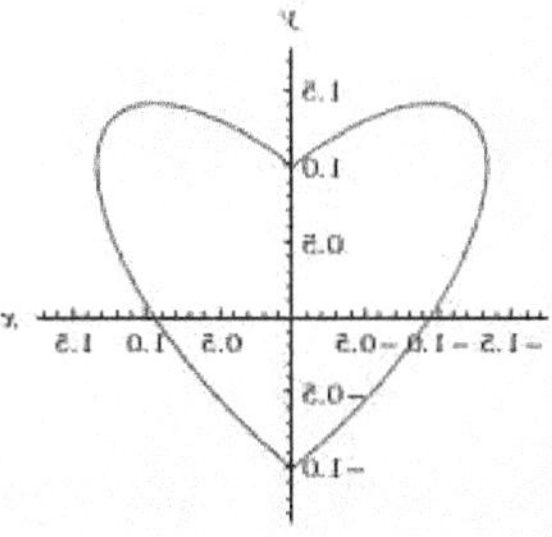

124

It's time to start making New Year's resolutions, but if the energy of revolution is present, we need to create revolutionary resolutions. There are three kinds of revolutions, those that are political, cultural, and consciousness. One changes politics and one changes culture, but they may not affect consciousness. A consciousness revolution affects both politics and culture. Talk of revolution doesn't have to bring up issues of fear as long as love has been consciously inserted into the conversation because love overcomes fear. Around the world, people are starting to wake up, which means a consciousness revolution is in fact happening. It would be great if it remained a spiritual awakening, but unless things change economically, it could become violent simply because the 'have nots' are awakening to the fact that they are expected to continue as slaves for the 'haves.' Awakening happens before action, which could come in the form of an angry response when enough pain has been created that it causes people to rebel, such as when you cut off the supply of goods and consumers say, "I'm going to do something about this," which could just mean buying up all of the toilet paper, or it could mean department stores being looted of everything they have. Before making your New Year's resolutions you should ask yourself, "What can I do to keep the energy of revolution peaceful?" The best resolution you can make is to commit to living love every day.

125

One massive social construct that's changing throughout the world is indigenous people standing up to voice, "Enough of the neglect and abuse, this is who we are and what we're about." They are responding to a new energy of revolution for social change because they are seeing themselves through a new set of eyes that allows them to remember what their ancestor taught, that they are great beings of light, and with that comes a sense of self-empowerment. We're going to see a lot more of this as those who were previously among those who 'don't have' are now standing up for an immediate change from those who 'do have' and are demanding a re-creation of the economy, equality, and justice because they now see themselves as worthy, as ready to benefit, and must have that recognition and respect. During the coming years, not just native tribes, but all of the minorities in a world in which the white patriarchy has dominated, will be a burst of change in social structures directed at these kinds of relationships, creating closer communities with less division, all because of courageous people willing to face the unknown to bring about change for the kind of society they want to experience. What sort of world do you want to live in? New Energies are coming into our awareness every day that will bring about this kind of change. When you set your intent with the Universe to create new and better paradigms, always remember to insert love into the equation.

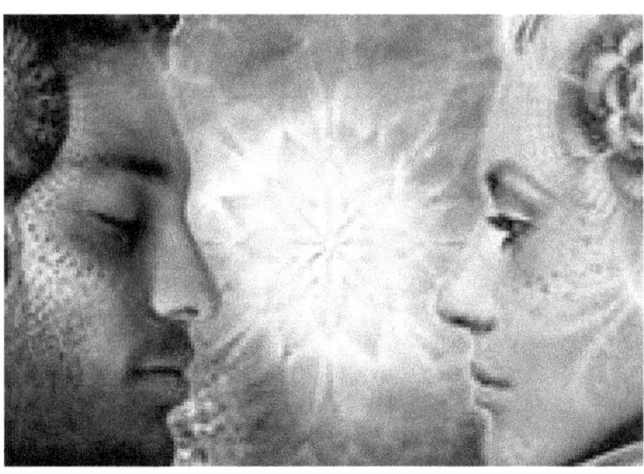

126

Old fear-based third-density structures have started to crumble away. Even those built of bricks that were solid and meant to last very long eventually give in to time, and ultimately, the bricks began to crumble as the mortar weakens. Earth's natural movements and shifting create enough friction to affect the crumbling even more. Major constructs of society will continue to crumble for several more years until those at the top come to realize the obvious, that all humans need recognition and respect. That's part of the consciousness revolution that's being presented at this time in history designed to straighten out the social ruts we've been in for so long, and instead create a whole New World based on love and compassion. It will never be this easy again for so many new paradigms to become our reality, but remember, out of chaos comes unlimited potential, and chaos is what most are experiencing. Feeling powerless creates the spark that ignites revolution because our soul seeks balance. You reach a point where you say, "I want my power back, I don't want this anymore." Revolution creates independence to say, "I don't want to go in that direction or think that way, I choose not to believe this." Those with economic power over others have been grooming humanity like cattle for hundreds of years, but the cows are waking up to all the bullshit, realizing they are so much more, and are preparing to knock down the fences of the owners if it is the only way to achieve a new kind of independence and whole new world. Please remember to take time to send energy to the world for peaceful change.

127

For a whole New World to become the consensus reality, you must become a standard, a role model for others to follow, as the one who displays an image of hope for all and who has within them the love and compassion needed at this time in history by always doing the best you can with what you have available to you at the moment, so use your resources wisely and to your best advantage. Humans have a history of hitting rock bottom before they rise up, plus they tend not to hear the message of hope until the noise gets really loud, but not everyone will be affected negatively by the illusion. Most will, but you don't need to. Still, at some point, the masses will realize there is just too much of a monetary gap between those who have and those who don't have, so a time will come to even things out, either voluntarily or by revolution. Start imagining what that transition will look like and begin sharing ideas to create peaceful change. A dam that is built upstream and kills everything downstream isn't the kind of world you want to live in, or where there are only enough resources for those living above the dam, but it's the kind of economy we have. There are sufficient resources on the planet for everyone, so become an activated activist and share your ideas for creating the kind of world that can provide for all of us.

128

Out of chaos comes unlimited potential. The pandemic opened many new doorways involving the economy and technology, but what we need most is world peace, which requires bringing an end to all wars. Countries on this planet have become so intermingled and codependent on each other that it is now impossible for any single country to change the world, other than for one country to declare war on all the others, which could happen. This world is not changing fast enough; therefore, we are seeing clouds of war brewing on the horizon. We must begin demanding world peace because massive change is about to happen, which will show up in either peaceful or destructive ways. Humanity can change itself peacefully. The world is ready to do it, but how it's done is our choice. We are reality creators; we weave our thoughts and beliefs together. Weave your own tapestry for the creation of a whole New World that has a loving and sustainable future, otherwise, you get woven into someone else's design that could hold a very catastrophic future. Don't be misled by those who are blinded by the illusion of power and try to manipulate you by shouting with the loudest voice.

Prana is lifeforce energy. It's in the air we breathe and holds the essence of Source within it. When it enters the body, intense hormones are secreted that do all kinds of things. Three of them have a strong effect on mood, those being dopamine, serotonin, and endorphins. Studies have found that those who have violent tendencies or try to commit suicide often lack these chemicals. Because of Prana, certain breathing techniques can alter our behavior by increasing the flow of these hormones, which creates a lucid state allowing you to temporarily shift out of the illusion. It's built into your physical system to do this. Yogis are trained to consciously modify their bodily chemicals, fully knowing they have a profound effect on behavior. Buddhist monks are naturally peaceful, not for the vows they take, but from doing breathing techniques. Instead of having a knee-jerk reaction, taking a deep breath creates an energy shift, which allows you to respond more clearly to a situation. You breathe in, hold, shift, then breathe out, and hold again. When you are in fear you immediately hold your breath. When you feel you're out of time you hold your breath. You can release fear and create more time by slowly breathing in and out. To bring an end to war on the planet and create world peace, all we must do is learn to breathe.

130

Were you ever traveling up a hill, only to find yourself in a line of cars behind an old truck that was chugging along and barely moving? That's what it's like right now for everything in the Universe because of what's happening here on Earth because humanity isn't moving fast enough. Our slow spiritual evolution is causing all the other aspects of the Universe to slow down. Everyone is watching us, patiently waiting for us to wake up to our true spiritual nature and become activated into service for the highest good of the Divine Plan. Each of us individually and as an entire species made a conscious choice to seek out the highest vibrational frequency we have available, which for this experience on Earth is to live love every day. Both the seen and unseen are doing all they can to get us to realize this simple truth and to begin working in the higher realms of conscious awareness. New energies are being sent to us at this time just for this specific reason. We need to stop seeing ourselves as separate from the rest of the Universe, and instead, become the love we were meant to be. Start raising your vibrational frequency. Take that old truck you're driving and give it a tune-up, or even better, trade it in for something new and stop slowing everyone else down.

131

Spiritual awakening happens when we realize there is so much more than what we see in front of us. Next, is to become activated into service for the highest good of all, which means to have the positive intent of Divine Feminine, then to give it wings by acting as a positive force in this world as Divine Masculine. An Activated Activist is one who is awake and acts with love, participating only in nonviolent revolution. They gather with numbers of like-minded people to protest peacefully or use social media as a nonviolent means to use their voice as leverage to bring change to countries and corporations that are more concerned with economic dominance in the world market than they are in regard to protecting the Earth. Just because a business sells something organic, it doesn't mean they don't have their money invested in something very lethal elsewhere. That's the nature of big business, so do your research. When you find something 'fishy' let them know and refuse to buy their products until the problem is corrected. Support small local companies and minority businesses, but make sure your money goes to places that fit your belief system. A successful rebellion requires more than just one person. Individually, you are not scary enough to corporate bullies, but when those of like thoughts work together in unity it gets to them. How we spend our money is a powerful tool that affects the corporate world, especially when large numbers of humans refuse to purchase a harmful product. This year, be part of a loving rebellion that supports your vision for the creation of a whole New World, and act with love.

132

The energy on the planet is moving faster than it ever has before and will continue to accelerate as we're faced with the challenges that are needed for the successful creation of a new Earth, things like viruses, A.I. technology, an equitable economy, housing, homelessness, war, abuses of human rights, Earth disasters, and racial injustice. Humanity has reached a midway point in its awakening for social change, so don't sit there in your roller coaster seat and scream. With just a few more years left to go, we are now beginning to see a bright light shining on the prospect of creating a whole New World. So take a deep breath, hold it for a moment, allow the energy to shift, then slowly breathe out, imagining the sacred breath of God, which it is. Then sit back and enjoy the ride as the roller coaster races downhill and makes its final loops. Then you can laugh with your hands in the air knowing you are safe, although you may see that others are still in panic. Just send them love so they can finally realize that it's all just an illusion they created.

133

Healing is a process of letting go of what you no longer identify with or that no longer matches the nature your frequency is resonating with. Your mind is a mixture of both your human self and your spiritual self. The higher you go in density, the less focus you have on your human, and likewise, the more you focus on your human, the more you will try to solve problems the human way, but that is a slow road and is not where humanity is going. Most of the problems we are now facing are multidimensional and therefore will require multidimensional answers, which is why we must learn to be in third, fourth, and fifth-density all at the same time. Nothing is black and white any longer, and nothing is either this or that, because duality has been lifted, but it doesn't mean there is now just one reality, it means that now there are many. Instead of choosing to be on the right or left, we must be able to see the entire spectrum of potential, so we must choose wisely by closely looking at all of the various perspectives involved, which can only be done by working together in unity. We want our new Earth to reflect the realm of Spirit, with attributes that are akin to enlightenment, self-awareness, and self-realization. That is the high road we must learn to follow, and at some point, it will become the acceptable norm for human behavior. When we can allow ourselves to become unstuck and freed from the limitations of our old beliefs, we will know the true meaning of healing.

134

Yes, it's all about you, but too much information is coming in and people are becoming overwhelmed, going crazy, and getting depressed. Don't start taking antidepressants because they tend to flatline your view of the world. To be mentally healthy it's important to be able to experience the highs and lows of life. With all of the new downloads your brain is receiving, and will continue to increase, to stay mentally healthy you must learn to let go and release as much of it as you can. Like computers, at times your mind needs to have the junk removed. When you receive a download, analyze it, experience it, and let it go. Don't hang on to it like a hoarder. Breathe in, hold, and then let it go. Once you've had an experience it's old information, so learn to clean up what's going on inside your mind, then you'll be able to handle the new downloads much better when they come in. Everything is just an illusion, so realize that a healthy mind is one that can consciously let go of the past, forgive the past, and move forward into the future.

135

Imagine for a moment that you've found a perfect flower and want to remember its beauty, so you take it home and put it into a vase, but soon the leaves wilt and the petals fall off. Your experiences in life and the way you remember them are often like the flower, but you enshrine those moments believing them to be the very best times of your life, or for some, the worst times of your life. Over time, your memory of it becomes less accurate until all you have is just a fragrance of the former experience, but you still believe it's how life should be because it was right and good, so you become depressed from grieving what is gone, but you're just fooling yourself because you're holding onto a belief and an image that no longer exists. This world is changing, and so are you. Some days will be wonderful, and others won't, then the very next day will be wonderful again. Don't hold onto what was or insist that life always remains the way you want it to. Don't get upset over imperfect experiences because it will cause you to miss the experience of what's happening now. There is great beauty to be found in fallen leaves and incredible power still found in faded flowers, but if all you're doing is trying to hold onto what was, you'll always be disappointed in what's going on now and will block out the potential for what could be.

136

Ancient Chinese teachings say that to become master one must first overcome a great adversary and although this opponent may appear to be your enemy, on a spiritual level, they are your best friend because they are teaching you things no one else can. On days when you feel like the world is against you, that it's just you, versus everyone else, realize it's a gift. You are being allowed to become a hero because you are facing such a great opponent. Every move you make, every thought you think, and every experience you have is teaching you something you're ready to learn, mostly about yourself, to finally let go of the child you once were and awaken to your full potential, but awakening can be hard because it requires facing the truth about you and your world, but will it be the red pill or the blue pill? Do you want to know the truth about the changes going on now or hang on to memories of what was? When you don't know what to do, just do the loving thing. Challenge the old world with the potential of what could be. Love those around you and yourself. All you need to succeed is to be a function of love in this now moment and show the world how love is supposed to work. Where love is, fear can't exist. A true master no longer has opponents.

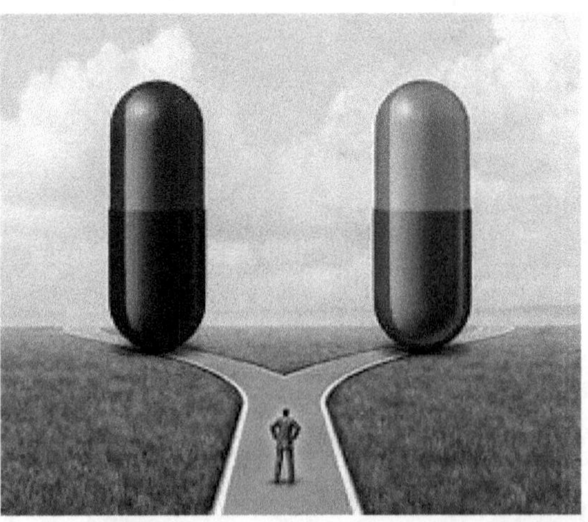

137

Some people say that we are here to shine our light into the world, but the problem is that while you're on Earth you are half-spirit and half-human. You didn't come here to be a monk on the mountain who just watches the world as it crumbles. No, you are here to help make it crumble in a peaceful, nonviolent way. This world is ready for major change more than ever before and nothing can hold it back, but we can be a factor in how it plays out. Energetically speaking, you already have within you all that's needed. You have the knowledge, strength, and previous successes to create a peaceful, loving transition. The times we are in are pivotal, so you must be in balance so that you don't fall every time the world shakes. It's time to be done with your trauma and drama. The spirit you are is here to allow love and light to flow into the world but that same powerful spirit chose to come here at this time of massive change to have a positive effect, however, you can't be your spirit self during all of your human experience, so to aspire to be a monk on the mountain is kind of useless in this day and age because you came here to jump in the sandbox and be part of the nitty-gritty, so the secret is to find the balance between your spiritual self and your human self.

138

Finding a balance between your human self and your spirit is the key to sanely functioning in this world. When you're in third density, all you see are reflections of yourself so it's easy to form attachments to the things you like because they give you a sense of security. As you come into fourth density, and ultimately into fifth, attachments to ego and worldly pleasures diminish, because without reflection and all the labels, you experience expansion. You feel less likely to take up a cause or carry the cross of a martyr. In third density, it's easy for compassion to be confused with feeling sorry for someone in which your actions are based on guilt for not having to suffer in the same way, but for those in the higher realms, true compassion is about honoring the path others choose. You feel them completely instead of making it all about you. Creating a new Earth shouldn't be a burden, a cause you must follow, or a cross you must carry. It should be something you are passionate about, like an artist, and something you want to do simply because you are a creator being with a vision who is choosing to create it, not out of guilt, remorse, or sorrow, but out of the love you hold for humanity.

139

True freedom is not what they teach us. All you experience and all you perceive as outside of you comes from within. Nothing can exist without your consciousness being present to perceive it, so everything you see in your 3-D world is a reflection of your internal Universe in one way or another. Even when someone who has a mental illness comes into your life and creates havoc, they are nothing but a mirror of something within you that's being triggered. All energy starts out as neutral until you attach labels to it. When you fear another person, in the bigger picture, what you are fearing is some sort of trauma within yourself. If you have no fear of such a thing and don't feed it with your negative emotions, it won't exist for very long. That's also the nature of power because it feeds off of fear. Those who are hungry for power must feed upon your fears regularly for them to survive. It's time to stop feeding government and corporate power-hungry animals who don't care anything about you other than to keep you in fear. The best way to do it is to release all of the fears you still carry within yourself. Freeing your mind from fear is the real meaning of freedom.

140

Freedom consciousness is about dying to the old human ways and transforming yourself into a new human by allowing the spirit you are to shine as you rise from the ashes of your old life, like the mythical Phoenix. Your Spirit is just pretending to be human, and it's time you acknowledged that! Still, there are those who want to be like a god over others by seeking power, but to truly be god-like one must have the experience of freedom. Power feeds off of the fears of humans, wants what someone else has, and takes it through fear, usually as cowards with a very loud voice. Seeking power creates limited thought within the illusion. They feel they can never get enough of power because it's not real. We are taught that power means freedom when it's really just the opposite because power leads to enslavement, especially when it comes to financial freedom, which should be a right, not some lofty dream for the very few, and can crumble at any moment. But power is just a small part of the problem we face within the self-created matrix we live in, which is a toxic cloud of fear-based beliefs that arise when we choose to remain focused on this third-dimensional reality. It's time to get off the merry-go-round and experience freedom consciousness.

141

Everything changes when you realize that the Universe isn't judging you for who you are or what you've done. Instead, humans judge you, and they only do that because you judge yourself. The human says, "What's the right thing to do," because you always want to be right. Spirit says, "What's the loving thing to do?" Ask that question instead, and many of the other choices disappear. We are not here to be right; we are here to be Light. Buddha explained that everything going on within the mind is dukkha, i.e. 'garbage.' It is all junk, your thoughts, issues, questions, and beliefs are like blinders on a horse that limit your ability to experience freedom consciousness. This limitation keeps you caged like an animal in the human zoo, forcing you to live within the walls of your self-made crystal prison, but when you get out of your brain and beyond all your fears and doubts, it raises your vibrational frequency. It shatters the walls of the prison and sets you free, then all you do is walk through it. The secret to becoming sane is to get beyond your mind and into the higher realms where 'the loving thing to do' is what guides you. Always ask yourself, "Who would Jesus bomb?"

142

Peace and war reflect your energy in regard to how much you love or how much you fear. When war comes in the name of peace or if fear shows up after claiming to be love, it's a wolf, not a sheep, so don't be fooled by it. But love is the higher vibration, so ultimately, love wins. It occupies the spaces of freedom consciousness, which is a constant state of peaceful, blissful expansion. The Buddhist teachings talk about a state of mind called Shunyata, which early translators defined as the void or emptiness, but Shunyata is actually a state of incredible fullness in which the crystal-clear light of consciousness is so full it appears to be empty, like a glass of water filled to the brim. It is a state of ease and grace beyond the mind where the illusion of duality does not exist. Most people don't believe that war on Earth will ever be ended, but the only wars that truly exist are those going on inside your mind, and you can end those wars by first acknowledging the darkness for what it is, which is usually a traumatized emotion that eventually became a belief, then go into that state of self-love called Shunyata and replace all of your old traumas with things you are passionate about, such as creating a whole New World. Stop trying to become enlightened without doing all of the work that's required and become enlightened now.

143

Enlightenment is nearly impossible to define because it's without limitation. It has no boundaries, borders, or barriers so the moment you try to define it, you limit it. One can only say, *it's kind of like this,* and describe its qualities and characteristics. For example, you could say, "Enlightenment is kind of like an open sky." It's hard to describe death because there is no actual death. When you leave your Earthly body you take on an energetic body and continue along your path as if going down the opposite side of the mountain into wholeness. Then you come up another mountain and back into separation, until you reach a point in your spiritual evolution and say, "I think I've had enough of this," which is your enlightenment. Most people have already had numerous past lives as some kind of holy person, so there's no longer any need to meditate for years in an ice cave, shave your head, put your hands in a prayer position, bow down, or prostrate yourself. Some holy men wear white robes or orange robes, Tibetans wear saffron robes, and Christian holy men wear black robes. In India, holy men wear a loincloth and smoke a lot of hashish. Trying to identify yourself as holy is garbage. Showing the world how holy you are by wearing a costume is just ego because enlightenment is kind of like standing before the world naked.

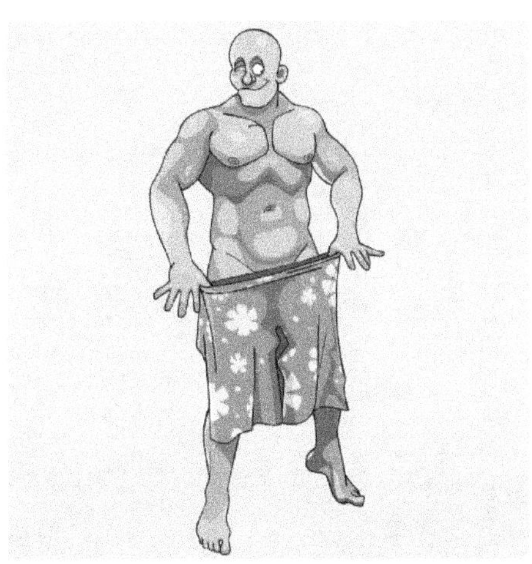

144

This is a story of how Buddha's teachings about enlightenment first came into existence. It is said that after Sidhartha had his realization, he walked through the forests experiencing his new sense of freedom and liberation from worldly matters in a state of bliss, with no desire to teach it, nor any desire not to teach it. He had no agenda whatsoever. On the seventh day, a former friend could see something was different and said, "What have you discovered?" His response was spontaneous, natural, and organic, not trying to impress, just answering the question. After explaining his realization he was *Buddha, the enlightened one.* What he spoke had nothing to do with heaven, hell, salvation, or sin, but just about why suffering exists, which later became known as the *Four Nobel Truths,* and said suffering could be ended by following the *Eightfold Path* of detachment and neutrality, and that inner peace and happiness could only be found from within, not from someone else or praying to God. Happiness cannot be found anywhere outside of you.

145

People are becoming traumatized from just watching the news, causing depression and suicide to be at an all-time high. The next series of posts are about enlightenment and terms like waking up, activation, and ascension. But enlightenment has to do with the life of Buddha so without some knowledge of that it's hard to understand. Buddha was born 500 years before Jesus and also had a miraculous birth. He was a young prince who left his home to discover why humans experience suffering. He attained his enlightenment at about the age of thirty after meditating for a very long time and taught his realization until his death at the age of eighty years old. His teachings were never intended to be a religion and didn't become so until after he died. What he taught was more like psychology, philosophy, or a way of life. Buddha was not a god and never claimed to be, just a man who discovered his inner self, something everyone can do. Buddhism emphasizes meditation, not to commune with God, but to study the mind. Buddhists have studied the mind for more than 2,500 years, which didn't begin in Europe until the coming of Sigmund Freud and Carl Jung a little over 100 years ago, so they understand the mind better. It's important to view enlightenment, not as some form of religious doctrine, but as a way to control your mind during times of chaos, rather than freaking out in fear or getting angry, and becoming depressed every time the world squeaks.

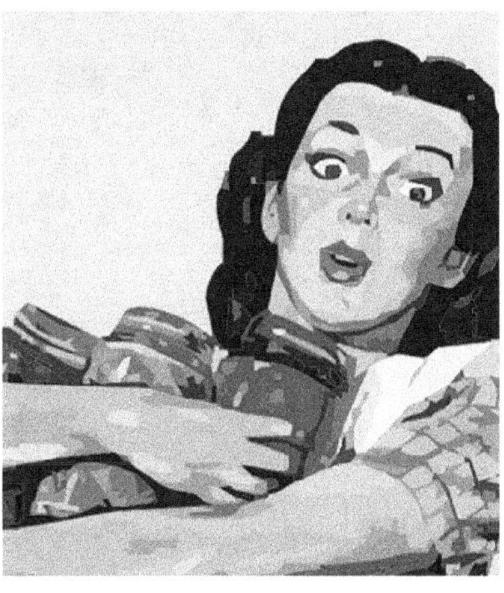

146

Enlightenment is not about becoming holy, following the beliefs of another, or being told what rewards you'll get if just do as you are told. That's just spiritual materialism, a seduction into the illusion of ego's playground rather than the truth about 'what' you are. Enlightenment is a release of your self-created ego that didn't exist before you were born and quickly dissolves after you die. Any sense of self-absorption or self-gratification are patterns of addictive behavior, and once you know those patterns, you must go beyond your mind, thoughts, beliefs, moods, and emotions. It requires that you transcend your humanness, but at the same time, be human. It's to be half-human and half-divine. Enlightenment is about expanding your awareness beyond time and space with the realization that everything in this world is an illusion. It's important to remember a human uses five senses to perceive reality, so everything you experience is extremely limited, but a Divine Human can sense so much more because they know there is so much more that is going on and that there are no limitations. It's important to always be fearless, impeccable, and open to all the unlimited possibilities.

147

Discussing enlightenment, Chögyam Trungpa Rinpoche once said, "The bad news is you're falling through the air with nothing to hang on to or even a parachute. The good news is, there is no ground." We want to rely on what feels solid, but freedom consciousness allows us to find comfort in knowing that everything changes, never just 'this or that.' There is no one answer to anything. Our lives are a multidimensional illusion, but enlightenment transcends the singularity of "who I am" to "what I am," and ultimately to "I Am." Enlightenment is an expansion of the human experience into multiplicity. It removes the labeling of your reality as good or bad, and instead to see the pure, clear light of consciousness, which is unconditional love. You are onto others and also onto yourself, becoming a truly authentic being without all of the energy feeding, manipulation, seeking power, or control. You become honest with yourself. If you're out of balance you make the corrections, integrating who you are with what you are, recognizing the spirit that you are while still in human form. Someday, you'll lose the form and move on to the next experience. By developing freedom consciousness, you come to realize you are so much more than you could ever imagine, a multidimensional being of light and love who has aspects residing in different realms, dimensions, and planes of existence all at once.

148

The most courageous thing anyone can do is to face the truth about themselves, to know what you're really made of, after that, you're on the way to experiencing the fun part, such as having a relationship with the higher aspects of yourself, trusting the Universe, and experiencing life on Earth with ease, grace, and joy. The thing about enlightenment is that it already exists within you. There is at least one aspect of your multidimensional self that is already fully realized, so although it feels as if you're on a journey as a seeker of truth, what you find is that you're already there. You discover a hidden illuminated treasure, your raised vibrational frequency, which by now is at its highest level. Freedom consciousness is the realization that you and the Universe have never been separated, so don't allow your enlightenment to separate you from others by creating just another ego trip. Remember, even those who live in a monastery must still wash the dishes and take out the garbage.

149

Traumas hidden within your subconscious create your shadow self, so as long as you are in 3-D, you will always have a Dark Side because of that duality, but you also have a choice, to ignore your darkness or face it. You can't consciously expand your awareness into the higher realms, i.e., 4-D and 5-D until you have faced those traumas and made peace with them. The acceptance of who you are allows what you are, (i.e. your spirit), to merge with your fragmented human and heal your inner woundings. When the spirit self and human self are able to come together in perfect union, it's like making love to yourself, which gives birth to a Divine Human. So admit it, man up, grow some balls, and face your inner shadows, aspects of you that were denied, held back, repressed, and shamed for years because you were taught they were wrong, sinful, or immoral. It may take years of searching before you allow these aspects to show themselves, but when they do, be authentic and accept 'who you are' without excuses or justification. Don't allow yourself to shine so brightly that you never get to see your shadows. Don't try to be something different or someone you are not because after all, wearing a robe or a cross doesn't make you any more holy, just as putting a feather in your ass doesn't make you a chicken.

150

Life was never meant to be so hard. When your mind and body are in alignment, you are in the flow of energy much like you see in nature. Water takes the easiest route, always going downhill, and lightning strikes the tallest object. Does either think about what they are doing? Life doesn't always make sense and we waste a lot of time trying to figure things out, but contradictions do occur, so learn to allow for that. Example: *if birds of a feather flock together, why do opposites attract?* Why can't both exist? You are both 'who you are' and 'what you are.' You are singular and multiple at the same time. Try this short mantra, *"I am one, you are one, we are one. I am you; you are me; we are one."* You are a multidimensional being with aspects of yourself that exist in other realms. When you allow them to be real, it creates a synergy of wholeness and balance. One of your aspects is who you pray to when you want to talk to God, so ask yourself this, "Do I identify with my human self, or do I choose to identify with my Divine Spiritual Self? Do I choose violence or non-violence? Will I continue to judge others, or can I commit to Divine Neutrality? Can I only find justice through revenge, or can I forgive the past and allow myself to move forward?" When you choose to love, it removes what is not love and puts you into the flow, so that the answers to life's questions come to you more easily.

Transformational Publishing
bypass the traditional publishing route
Online market
Author
Literary agent
publisher
market
writes a few chapters, marketing proposal, queries literary agents
reviews proposal, pitches to publishers
edits, cover design, layout, marketing, ad campaign, publicity
bookstores sell books
I LOVE TO WRITE
Transformational Publishing
Transformational Publishing.com